ADVANCE PRAISE

"Just as Hephaestus forges and Prometheus shares, Ivan has struck again with precision, imparting complex knowledge about artificial intelligence and making it accessible to the average person.

"As AI continues to grow exponentially, it's easy to be left behind, but Pandora's Pivot offers a practical roadmap on how we can become a better leader and problem solver through artificial intelligence.

"Framed through the lens of Greek mythology, the book not only equips readers with the technical depth and skills to collaborate and grow organizations effectively with AI, but also encourages deeper reflection on how we, as individuals and organizations, choose to wield this transformative power. Rather than treating AI as gods to worship, Ivan positions it as a tool: one that, when used wisely, can unlock extraordinary creativity, productivity and purpose-driven innovation."

NATALIE LOI
Award Winning Tech Designer
Successful People of Malaysia & Singapore
Australian High Commission awarded Young Entrepreneur
Women in Tech APAC Awards Most Impactful Initiative Award Finalist

"Ivan's tsunami warning – AI will flatten the human hierarchy of corporate leadership when everyone can be an authentic miniaturized Pandora (AMP), farewell beguiling solo CEO, now reborn and empowered with 'Advanced-Man-Power' – the next Pandora Pivot's Delta δ."

PROFESSOR ANTHONY SC TEO
Chevalier of the Order Palmes Académique
Academician Leading Univer-Cities Talent Magnet in Four Volumes, 2013-2025

"Pandora's Pivot is a rare achievement – an intellectually rich, morally grounded, and deeply accessible guide to the age of AI. Just as Pandora's curiosity unleashed both chaos and hope upon the world, agentic AI opens a new era of possibility and peril. The challenge before us is not simply to open the box, but to steward its contents with wisdom, foresight and moral clarity. By blending mythological narrative with modern technological insight, this book empowers readers not only to understand agentic AI, but to lead with it. Business leaders will walk away fluent in AI fundamentals, equipped to collaborate with technical teams, and ready to harness AI's creative and strategic potential across their organizations. A timely and transformative read."

PROFESSOR ANDY CHUN
Leading AI Scientist, Hong Kong

"Very well written and concise and detailed! Well done."

PATRICK TSANG
Author, *The Global Citizen*
Chairman of the Tsangs Group and the Hong Kong Ambassadors Club (HKAC)

"This book presents what initially appears to be a lighthearted retelling of ancient Greek mythology, reimagining gods and demigods as flawed, relatable humans navigating their extraordinary powers. Yet beneath this engaging narrative lies something far more profound – a sophisticated exploration of artificial intelligence through the lens of timeless mythological themes.

"The author skillfully uses these ancient stories as a gateway to examine our most pressing questions about AI development and implementation. Rather than drowning readers in technical jargon, they pose fundamental questions about power, responsibility and the future of human-machine relationships through deeply human storytelling.

"As a Greek reader, I was particularly moved by how an Asian author could capture and reproduce our mythological heritage with such authenticity and respect. It's a beautiful reminder that despite geographical distances, we share common stories and universal concerns about power, hubris and progress.

"The book's greatest strength lies in making complex AI ethics accessible without sacrificing depth. By grounding futuristic concerns in ancient wisdom, the author creates a framework that feels both timeless and urgently relevant.

"I highly recommend this book – it's original, insightful and thought-provoking in all the right ways."

DR ELEFTHERIA EGEL
Social Entrepreneur
Startup Advisor
Board Member
Scholar, Berlin, Germany

"Pandora's Pivot *is an essential resource for leaders steering through the AI revolution. It brilliantly simplifies intricate AI ideas using the captivating narrative of Greek mythology, ensuring accessibility for non-technical professionals. This book equips leaders to communicate adeptly with technical teams, harness AI for innovation, and develop strategic plans that maximize its impact. A must read for visionary executives and policymakers aiming to harness AI for national and organizational advancement in today's digital age."*

MICHAEL ONG
Goodwill Ambassador and Special Envoy for Investment and Trade (Asia) to the President of the Republic of Timor-Leste

"Pandora's Pivot *is a remarkable and thought-provoking work that masterfully intertwines ancient myth with modern dilemmas, guiding readers through a captivating journey across values, leadership, wisdom, trust, and the ethical challenges of intelligent technologies. With eloquence and depth, the author reimagines timeless stories – from Pandora to Prometheus, Athena and beyond – as powerful metaphors for today's age of agency and artificial intelligence. Each chapter offers both narrative richness and practical insight, empowering readers to reflect, adapt and thrive amid uncertainty. This book stands out as both an intellectual treasure and an essential guide for anyone seeking clarity and purpose in an era of relentless change. An inspired achievement that will resonate with leaders, innovators and lifelong learners alike."*

DR WENDY LIEW
Adjunct Professor
Image and Management Brand Specialist
Keynote & TEDx Speaker

"Chapter 5 detonates like thunder in a silent sky. One moment, you're swept into the primal fury of Kronos and Zeus – Titans clawing for dominion. The next? You're staring into the soul of today's AI revolution. DeepSeek's open-source lightning ... OpenAI's empire-building ... trillion-dollar boardrooms where futures are forged in ambition and code.

"Then – genius strikes. Just as you brace for cold disruption ... the chapter reveals the secret weapon of tomorrow's victors. Not bigger models. Not faster chips.

"Intelligent. Revolutionary. Kindness.

"At Techlution, we live this truth: turning $2B supply chains into symphonies of efficiency ... scaling mental health rescue with AI that hears despair before it breaks ... winning client loyalty because we care as fiercely as we compute. This chapter? It's our battle-tested playbook.

"Leaders, visionaries, warriors of the new age: if you think AI's about algorithms alone, you're Kronos, blind.

"But fuse humanity with horsepower?

"YOU. RULE. OLYMPUS."

JERRY TSANG
Chief Commercial Officer, Techlution (Nasdaq: $ATGL)
Where AI Meets Human Courage

Published by
LID Publishing
An imprint of LID Business Media Ltd.
LABS House, 15–19 Bloomsbury Way,
London, WC1A 2TH, UK

info@lidpublishing.com
www.lidpublishing.com

A member of:

BPR ❀
businesspublishersroundtable.com

© Ivan Yong, 2025
© LID Business Media Limited, 2025

ISBN: 978-1-917391-50-4
ISBN: 978-1-917391-51-1 (ebook)

Cover and page design: Caroline Li

PANDORA'S PIVOT

A PRIMER FOR LEADING IN
AN AI-DRIVEN WORLD

IVAN YONG

MADRID | MEXICO CITY | LONDON
BUENOS AIRES | BOGOTA | SHANGHAI

DEDICATION

To God Almighty and Jesus Christ for the
grace to write this book, to my wife Nancy for
her unwavering belief in me; and to my parents,
who taught me that books are miracles.

CONTENTS

Acknowledgements   x

Foreword   xiii

Message from the Author   1

Chapter 1: Pandora's Pivot (Values & Purpose)   6

Chapter 2: Prometheus' Favour (Distributed Leadership)   34

Chapter 3: Athena's Wisdom (Wisdom & Discernment)   70

Chapter 4: The Dutiful Hephaestus (Trust)   98

Chapter 5: The Clash of the Titans (Intelligent Kindness)   130

Afterword   158

References   160

Blurb   168

Author Biography   169

ACKNOWLEDGEMENTS

Pandora's Pivot is a labour of love and grace.

I give thanks to God Almighty and Jesus Christ for the grace, the unearned favour and talent to write it. Many a times, when I struggled to write, I was led to books or Bible verses that would show me the path to continue on. Often it would lead to many more exciting discoveries which I curated and shared within the pages of this book.

Again, I am forever grateful to my muse and my wife, Nancy, for her quiet force in supporting my work. Her faith in me kept me going whenever I doubted myself. I relied on her confidence in me when I was approached to write *Pandora's Pivot*. She has, time and again, acquiesced to many of my outlandish ideas, which I have aplenty but little courage to embark on. This book exists because she believed it could.

I am also eternally indebted to my parents, especially my dearly departed father, who instilled within me and my siblings a cherished love of reading and an abiding joy in the pursuit of honest, hardworking endeavours.

Special thanks to:

Professor Anthony Teo, my mentor of two decades who regaled me with his knowledge of Ancient Greece and how it could continue to guide us in modern times.

Professor Cecilia Chan, for being a role model and a mentor in the pursuit of transformative innovation with AI, backed by research.

Professor Andy Chun, for sharing his expertise in AI and how art can be the catalyst of creativity for even technologists and engineers.

Tan Sri Dato' Sri Ir. Dr Sahol Hamid bin Abu Bakar, for his trust in me to help educate the next generation of Malaysians through my appointment as an Adjunct Professor with UNITAR.

Badrie Abdullah, who provided me with the means to contribute back to my beloved country, Malaysia, through TalentCorp, Malaysia.

Professor David Lane, for his trust in my ability to expand the body of knowledge in coaching and mentoring.

Dr Eleftheria Egel, who has shown me the nuts and bolts of conducting research in coaching and mentoring.

Dr Wendy Liew, for her confidence and partnership in translating business experiences into practical insights and knowledge.

Michael Ong, for his encouragement and inspiration to pursue my dreams.

Dr Juan Carlos Astudillo, who shares my goal in creating impact for the betterment of our society through technology.

Patrick Tsang, who inspires me with his tenacity and his belief that "anything is possible."

Kelvin Liu, who shares my enthusiasm in harnessing the innovative prowess of technology.

Hoh Jee Eng, who persistently supports my endeavours in fostering connections between Hong Kong and Malaysia.

All at LID Publishing for your belief in me, and your wonderful support in bringing this book to fruition: Martin Liu, Aiyana Curtis, Caroline Li and Teya Ucherdzhieva.

A special acknowledgement is extended to Alec Egan of LID Publishing, who first saw the possibility of *Pandora's Pivot*, after just an hour of chat over the phone. His continuous support and coaching has made writing this book an absolute joy.

FOREWORD

It is with genuine pleasure that I introduce *Pandora's Pivot*, a remarkable work that bridges the ancient wisdom of mythology with the real-world challenges of artificial intelligence (AI) in organizational leadership. This book arrives at a pivotal moment when AI is no longer a distant concept but a transformative force reshaping how we lead, collaborate and innovate across all sectors.

As someone deeply engaged in the intersection of AI, education and leadership, I have witnessed first-hand the need for non-technical professionals, especially leaders, to develop a robust understanding of AI's fundamentals. This book meets that need by offering readers a unique narrative framework rooted in Greek mythology, making complex AI concepts accessible, engaging and deeply relevant to practical business challenges. It gives a different perspective via this lens.

AI is often described as a double-edged sword, a Pandora's box of potential and peril. Through my work and my involvement in global AI literacy initiatives, I have learned that the true impact, much like the title of the book, depends on how leaders choose to harness it.

To lead effectively in an AI-driven world, leaders need to acquire AI literacy by first mastering the fundamentals and then engaging in continuous learning of this evolving technology. AI literacy is the essential communication skill empowering business leaders to foster creativity, productivity and innovation within their organizations.

Pandora's Pivot also invites leaders to re-examine the current leadership practices that may not be in sync with the technological powers of AI. Just as the concept of education is undergoing a transformative reevaluation, so too must we reassess the outdated concepts and business practices of the past.

I warmly recommend *Pandora's Pivot* to all professionals seeking to lead confidently and creatively in the AI era. By combining the insights of Greek mythology with practical AI knowledge, this book offers an invaluable guide to navigate the complex landscape of AI-enabled leadership and organizational psychology.

Prof Cecilia Ka Yuk Chan
Professor, Faculty of Education
Director, AI in Education Lab
The University of Hong Kong
July 2025

MESSAGE FROM THE AUTHOR

Artificial intelligence, or AI, has taken our world by storm. Knowledge, once a prized possession that separated the elite from the eager, now flows freely, stripped of its scarcity and liberated into the public domain. With a short prompt, AI conjures novels, art and films flawlessly and instantaneously. What took many years of learning, training and apprenticeship to produce is now condensed to a keystroke.

Yet, I believe all is not lost. While the world obsesses over AI's 'intelligence,' I wrote this book to confront the urgent need to draw our attention to the 'artificial' in AI. It might seem unconventional, but AI's true power is harnessed through its artificiality and not its intelligence. Allow me to explain.

While AI is now seeing rapid advancement, with some even predicting that AI will soon surpass human intelligence with Artificial General Intelligence (AGI), the adoption of AI in the market is sluggish. Business leaders, managers and organization decision makers are convinced that AI will alter the dynamics of almost every industry, but not many are able to articulate how.

Over the past ten years of my practice as an organizational psychologist and coach, I've witnessed how top business leaders leverage technology's potential. Their success lies not in mastering the technology itself, but in grasping its core principles, concepts and tools; while recognizing transformative capabilities of its applications. I call this type of mastery 'fluency in AI' or 'being fluent in the language of AI.'

When writing this book, I was looking at the subject matter with three lenses. First, from a position of hard sciences – I graduated with a degree in engineering from Nanyang Technological University in Singapore, which is ranked twelfth in the QS World University Ranking (2026). I have a keen eye for seeking solutions in technology that are simple to operationalize. Second, from a position of social sciences, organizational development in particular. I hold an MSc degree in organizational psychology from Birkbeck College, University of London, a leading teaching and research university in organizational psychology in the UK and Europe. To add to the former, I am currently an applied psychology PhD candidate at the University of Nottingham Malaysia with a research focus on AI and coaching. Third, from a position of a practicing organizational development consultant, coach and mentor. I am currently serving as Co-President Asia and Pacific of the European Mentoring and Coaching Council (EMCC).

The book I have written presents a unique perspective in the world of AI that is not overtly technical, yet presents many practical arguments for 'soft' uses of AI tools across disciplines and business functions.

Also, this book will give you enough technical knowledge and insights into the potential practical application of AI in business and organizational development. When you read this book, you will be able to:

- Become fluent in the language of AI, developing the ability to leverage its transformative capabilities and assess its influence.
- Master the fundamentals of AI and continuously enhance your knowledge to remain current with rapidly evolving technology.
- Solve bigger problems in the business and organizational context.
- Communicate more effectively with your technical teams to clearly articulate the solutions you wish to develop as a business leader.
- Enhance productivity and creativity in addressing business challenges through AI.
- Engage in insightful discussions with colleagues, understanding AI's potential impact across various organizational departments.

Finally, I have endeavoured to make learning fun through storytelling. In *Pandora's Pivot*, I have drawn inspiration from Greek mythology to set the theme for each chapter. I hope you'll enjoy reading the book as much as I have spent crafting it.

HOW TO USE THIS BOOK

My suggestion is for you to read the book twice:

1. Read the book from cover to cover in the order that is presented. If you are interested in the technical part of AI, spend more time on the section titled 'The AI Conundrum,' found in every chapter.

2. Next, keep the book readily available at your desk. And when you encounter any issues or are looking for new inspiration in the use of AI, read Chapter 5: The Clash of the Titans again. Chapter 5 will then guide you to what other chapters you should be reading thereafter.

You may also be led to do some desktop research or to use AI tools to help you generate ideas for the solutions that you might need. This time, however, you will be the master, exerting the full value of AI for your own purposes.

As AI is an evolving technology, I have a created a newsletter to allow us to continue our conversation and help us unlock its full potential. Join me by subscribing to the *Pandora's Pivot* newsletter at https://pandoraspivot.substack.com and I look forward to connecting with you soon.

Last but not least, I would like to thank you for procuring this book and spending your precious time reading my words, which I have curated for your success.

I firmly believe that history will recognize this era of AI expansion as a pivotal moment for humanity. I congratulate you for stepping forward not only to participate but to decisively influence the future of AI for generations ahead.

Blessings always.

CHAPTER 1
PANDORA'S PIVOT
(VALUES & PURPOSE)

"Beware, my brother, of gifts from Zeus!" thundered Prometheus.

"You are overthinking it, my dear brother, Prometheus," came a casual reply from Epimetheus, whose name bore the meaning of 'afterthought.'

"You are truly living up to your name, god of forethought," Epimetheus added.

"You think too much, overanalysing what is a simple truth: Zeus has come to his senses and has realized what a genius we are in our creation of man."

"You ought to savour this moment of victory over Zeus. This will echo not only in the Halls of Mount Olympus but will ring incessantly like a spear in the ears of all the Olympians."

"Let them see for themselves what we Titans are made of!"

"Zeus was fortunate that you and I had stood on his side, against our very own kind. If we had not done so, the Titans would have ruled for eternity," Epimetheus scoffed.

Prometheus could only shake in dismay as he knew his words would fall onto deaf ears. Epimetheus, the embodiment of reckless impulsivity, had once again given in to his nature; mindlessness.

Memories surged unbidden in Prometheus' mind.

It was not very long ago, when the brothers were tasked with the creation of man, that Epimetheus had carelessly endowed all vital traits to the animals, such as fur to keep warm, wings to soar in hunt, and the cunning art of disguise to cloak predators and prey alike. By the time Epimetheus turned to mankind, the well of gifts had run dry, leaving man vulnerable and exposed. It was Prometheus who had taken pity on man, his creation, when he defied Zeus to steal fire, which gave man a chance to thrive.

"Whatever it is. If it is from Zeus, return it at once! We shall have no share in what Zeus has to offer."

"Have you not seen how Zeus plotted against his father, Kronos?"

Zeus had plotted with his mother, Rhea, to overthrow Kronos, and now reigned as the unchallenged king of the gods, ruling over all the realms – the sky, the sea and even the underworld.

"And what woes did Zeus bring to his own father? Eternal condemnation in the depths of Tartarus; the deep, gloomy abyss of undying torment and suffering in the underworld!" Prometheus raised his voice, striking his fist into his open palm like a thunderclap.

"My brother, you are again overthinking the issue. Have you not seen whom Zeus asked to bring this gift to us – Hermes himself!" Epimetheus replied with a resounding voice of confidence.

"So what if Hermes delivered the gift?"

"Hermes, the messenger of the gods himself! And he has brought not only the gift but words of favour and flattery to our ears. It's a sure sign that this is a gift of honour."

"Epimetheus, we must not let our guard down, especially from Hermes, the master who pours honey into our ears!"

"I, for once, disagree with you, my brother. The gift is mine to keep. Besides, we have not seen anything like her. And she has a name – Pandora."

Epimetheus, ever the fool, had accepted Pandora, a gift from Zeus, wrapped in beauty and danger. Prometheus' warnings had been sharp and clear, but they were no match for his brother's thoughtless nature. He had a foreboding hunch as to what was to come, yet he was powerless against his brother's foolishness.

As he gazed at his brother, who stood oblivious and consumed by the beauty and charm of Pandora, Prometheus felt a bitter mix of frustration and sorrow. Epimetheus' mindlessness was not just a flaw, it was a force of destruction, a storm that would destroy all that he had created. And once again, Prometheus would bear the weight of his brother's mistakes.

———————

Pandora was a breath of fresh air. The first of her kind, a woman. Never seen before even by the creator of man: Prometheus himself. She looked like the men that Prometheus had created but yet in many ways more attractive, more beguiling.

Grudgingly, Prometheus agreed with his brother. Pandora seemed like a gift of honour and it was only fitting that a Titan, such as Epimetheus, be the one to marry her. Fashioned by Hephaestus, the god of fire and the forge, craftsmanship and sculpture, Pandora was perfect in every way.

Pandora was also endowed with many gifts from the gods.

Aphrodite, the goddess of love and beauty, breathed life into her and all the arts of love; Athena, the goddess of war and wisdom, clothed her, accentuating her beauty and taught her to be deft with her hands; Hermes, the messenger of the gods, schooled her in the mastery of not only her words but that of her mind; Poseidon, the god of the sea, brother to Zeus, bestowed on her a pearl necklace that would prevent her from drowning; Apollo, the god of music, taught her to play the lyre and to weave enchanting, soul-stirring melodies with her voice; and last but not least,

Hera, queen of the gods, goddess of marriage and women, wife to Zeus, bestowed upon her the most treacherous gift of all: an insatiable curiosity.

And so it came to pass that Pandora, the most beautiful maiden of her age, created by the gods, and adorned with their finest gifts, embodied the very essence of her name – 'all gifted,' a divine offering to mankind. With grace and beauty matching only the gods, she was whisked away by Hermes, to meet her husband, Epimetheus, as a peace offering between Zeus and the brothers.

Yet, beneath her radiant beauty and divine blessings lay a fateful secret, one that would unravel the threads of humanity's innocence, for Zeus had given her a final gift: a beautifully crafted box.

———————

Marriage was a bliss for both Epimetheus and Pandora. They were deeply in love, and as they whiled away time in each other's company, Pandora's thoughts kept drifting back to the box, the final parting gift from Zeus.

"This is my final gift to you, my dear child. A beautifully crafted box, made by Hephaestus, just for you." Zeus smiled as he presented the box to Pandora.

"Every detail is crafted to my instructions. Look at how intricate the designs are. Aren't they wonderful?"

"Yes, Zeus, they are. The box is so beautiful." Pandora tried to hide her delight with a small whisper in reply.

"Now child, the box is yours, with only one condition."

"What is it, Zeus?"

"You shall not open it. Ever."

"Why? Are the contents of the box dangerous?"

"No need to worry about what's inside, Pandora. There is nothing of interest that should concern you. Now go, my child, to meet your destiny!"

The conversation with Zeus continued to play on her mind since the day she joined Epimetheus as his beloved wife. Her thoughts kept drifting back to the box, its mysterious presence tugging at her mind like a shadow that clung to her every thought, a riddle begging to be unravelled.

Finally, curiosity got the better of Pandora. She was no longer able to shake away the nagging feeling that demanded her attention with every breath that she drew. The box, once a mere object of admiration, now seemed to call to her, its secrets whispering ever louder. She was now convinced that there was more than the eye could behold: the box must hold something precious, something rare, something befitting Zeus.

Her resolve was faltering.

"Zeus must have hidden something precious in the box," she spoke to herself.

"And since Zeus gave me the box as a wedding gift, that would mean that all that the box contains is mine too!"

Thoughts, once silent, now spilled into words, and words were the magic that moved the heart.

Before long, Pandora found herself reaching for the box and touched it, her fingers trembling as she traced the intricate patterns carved into its surface. Her fingers lingered, while she reconsidered her choice.

"What harm could it possibly do, to just open the box and take a peek at what is hidden inside?

"What is there to fear? Zeus said the box holds nothing of significance. Nothing of worth." Pandora now engaged in an intense soliloquy.

"Just one look," she murmured to herself. "And I shall be curious no more."

Her fingers tightened around the lid and, with a sharp intake of breath, she began to lift it – slowly, gingerly, for she feared that Zeus may find out.

First, a sharp, sinister hiss pierced the air, followed by a swirling mist, spreading, rushing to escape the box like a trapped animal. It surged and writhed, desperate to escape its confines, gathering strength as it rushed past Pandora.

And then came the smell.

It was an odour most foul, so utterly repugnant, that bore the stench of decay, of evil, of corruption, that choked all her senses, causing her to stagger back in horror.

Out of the depths of the box poured forth *Ponos* (hardship), *Limos* (starvation), *Algos* (pain), *Dysnomia* (anarchy), *Pseudea* (lies), *Neikea* (quarrels), *Amphilogiai* (disputes), *Makhai* (wars), *Hysminai* (battles), *Androktasiai* and *Phonoi* (manslaughters and murders).

Death, sickness, greed, hatred and the ills of the world had arrived. They would never leave.

The lives that men had known would change forever. They had led a carefree life and had been given dominion through the gift of fire by Prometheus. That came to an abrupt end. Zeus had exacted his revenge: bringing suffering to the cherished creation of Prometheus.

Realizing her folly, Pandora shut the lid of the box with much haste. Unbeknownst to her, she had trapped a small but vital light to guide humanity through the darkness that she had brought forth: *Elpis* (hope).

THE AI CONUNDRUM

With all the divine gifts bestowed upon her by the gods, Pandora was granted something far greater, something that would change the fate of mankind: the power of agency. For the decision to open the box lay neither with the gods, Prometheus and Epimetheus, nor the man they created, but with Pandora. Pandora had acted with free will, deliberating the decision within herself with no need for consultation with anyone.

Similar to Pandora, who once held the power to alter the fate of humanity, artificial intelligence has now achieved agency: the power that transcends mere computational automation but also the realm of autonomy. Furthermore, at the point of writing, AI has now entered the age of 'multi-agency' or what is known as a 'Multi-Agent System' (MAS). The visionary musings of Alan Turing, who once speculated, "It seems probable that once the machine thinking had started, it would not take long to outstrip our feeble powers ... They would be able to converse with each other to sharpen their wits," have now come to pass.

If you, my dear reader, began to conjure up an image of several Pandoras, opening multiple boxes or even began to deliberate among themselves on the merit of opening their boxes, you are sharing the same thoughts as mine. Disaster awaits, and what are our chances if we are not involved in that decision-making process?

However, before we jump to this conclusion, it would be beneficial to understand the origins of this new 'intelligence' that has now been bestowed with agency – known as 'agentic AI.'

Much like Pandora, who captivated both mortals and gods with her charm and brilliance when she was first shown to the world, the arrival of AI captivated our imagination with possibilities and dreams. The advent of 'machine learning,' a branch of AI that enabled computer systems to learn and perform tasks by being 'trained' with data, is akin to Pandora being bestowed with the wisdom of Athena.

Prior to this, in what is now known as 'classical AI,' a human programmer was needed to write an algorithm, a sequence of instructions to accomplish a certain task. AI was simply a design by a human programmer, and through the manipulation of symbols and using logical reasoning to represent knowledge, problems could be solved. In short, classical AI focused on explicit representations of knowledge and rule-based reasoning.

An example of this is 'Deep Blue,' the IBM chess-playing AI that defeated world champion Garry Kasparov in 1997. The chessboard, pieces and all possible moves were represented in Deep Blue using symbolic data structures. The rules of chess were introduced as a form of rule-based reasoning, aided by human chess experts on the strategic and tactical knowledge of the chess system. Deep Blue then used a 'minimax algorithm with alpha-beta pruning' technique to explore millions of possible moves and countermoves. Deep Blue did not learn from data or improve through playing experience. The defeat of Garry Kasparov was made possible entirely from pre-programmed rules and mathematical computation.

While the win was celebrated as a major milestone in the development of AI, it also saw a paradigm shift in the understanding and approach to AI development. The lack of learning ability, reliance on the acquisition and encoding of human knowledge into classical AI and the issue of scalability, prompted a dramatic shift into the space of 'statistical AI,' which set the foundation for the 'agentic AI' that we are seeing today.

At the heart of statistical AI lies a powerful technique known as 'machine learning,' where vast amounts of data are harnessed to train AI models to perform tasks without the explicit need of programming. The most sophisticated type of machine learning is known as 'deep learning,' which requires minimal intervention by the human programmer. The AI models used in deep learning are 'artificial neural networks,' designed to emulate the intricate workings of the human brain, unlocking unprecedented power in pattern recognition, decision-making and problem-solving. The fusion of data-driven machine learning and the mimicry of the human brain AI model has propelled AI into the next frontier that we all recognize now as large language models (LLMs).

LLMs are AI models that process natural language with the ability to understand and generate human-like text, a form of 'generative AI.' While LLMs are a generally new technological advancement, generative AI can be traced back to Joseph Weizenbaum, who created ELIZA, a chatbot, in 1961, the first historical example of generative AI. Generative AI is a form of AI models that are trained to recognize patterns and structures within their data training, enabling them to generate new content based on natural language prompts.

In 2022, OpenAI released ChatGPT, a groundbreaking LLM that launched the age of generative AI. ChatGPT not only demonstrated unprecedented capabilities in understanding and generating human-like text, it was able to assist, create and innovate across different industries. From composing poetry to writing programming codes, all it requires is a text prompt from a human. It was almost like engaging AI in a conversation to create and innovate. As of January 2025, ChatGPT boasts 300 million active users per week with ten million paying subscribers and is valued at an impressive US $157 billion, reflecting its significant impact on the tech industry and its growing user base.

Due to the rapid advancement of LLMs, which process natural language, and now large multimodal models (LMMs), which can process multiple types of data such as text, images, video and audio, AI is now at the nascent stage of the next major leap: agentic AI.

WHAT IS AGENTIC AI?

NVIDIA, the Californian-based chip designer, which provides the hardware that powers various forms of AI, including that of ChatGPT, describes agentic AI as a form of AI that "uses sophisticated reasoning and iterative planning to autonomously solve complex, multi-step problems."

Much like Pandora, who reasoned continuously with herself on the merit of opening Zeus' box, agentic AI is capable of engaging in the same reasoning, weighing options and solving problems. The similarity goes even deeper. Just as Pandora ultimately acted on her reasoning, agentic AI will also eventually act on its reasoning and iterative planning. In both cases, the power of agency drives action, for better or worse, shaping outcomes in ways that ripple far beyond the moment of decision.

And one final commonality: humans are not involved in either the deliberations or the execution of those deliberations.

NVIDIA explained that an agentic AI or AI agent uses a four-step process for problem-solving:

- **Perceive**: The AI agent is capable of gathering and processing data from various sources, such as databases, sensors or digital interfaces.
- **Reason**: The AI agent will understand the task, generate the solutions and coordinate specialized AI models to execute those solutions such as content creation and more.
- **Act**: The AI agent executes tasks based on the plans it formulated through integration with external tools and software.
- **Learn**: The AI agent 'learns' and continuously improves through a process known as 'data flywheel,' where data generated from its interactions are fed back into the system to improve the model.

While Pandora may have learned quickly from her action that she had done harm to humanity, closed the lid with all her might never to open it again, an AI agent is also capable of the same learning and adaptability while engaged in a task.

In a forward-looking white paper titled, "Navigating the AI Frontier: A Primer on the Evolution and Impact of AI Agents" by the World Economic Forum in collaboration with Capgemini, it was highlighted that AI agents have undergone remarkable transformation since the 1950s, when they were first developed. The early AI agents were characterized by deterministic behaviour, highly dependent on a basic rule-based system that made them predictable and without the 'learning' ability.

As discussed earlier, AI agents are now sophisticated autonomous entities, characterized by non-deterministic behaviour, capable of executing complex decision-making tasks and managing uncertainty to achieve desired outcomes. Typically, these are known as either goal-based or utility-based agents.

Goal-based agents are designed to achieve a predefined goal or goals and will have within their capacity to make complex decisions that will lead them to attaining those goals. Built within them are goal-planning algorithms, giving them the ability to consider whether their actions will take them closer to their objectives or not. If not, the agent will revisit the decision-making until a better probability outcome is found. For example, a sales chatbot with a goal to prospect a certain number of prospects will plan the necessary sales tactics that will help it achieve the goal set. In the process, it will revise its actions based on the outcome, giving the agent a learning ability.

On the other hand, utility-based agents are much more sophisticated than goal-based agents, as they are deployed to handle tasks that lack a straightforward outcome such as attaining a predefined goal. Essentially, what utility-based agents do is to consider each potential state and give it a weighted score. This allows for optimal decision-making, especially in a scenario where several conflicting goals are set. An example would be an autonomous driving vehicle that optimizes safety while balancing speed, fuel consumption and safety.

At the core of the architecture of these AI agents is the 'control centre,' which performs several crucial steps that manage the flow of information from input to desired output. The steps are:

- user inputs
- decision-making and planning
- memory management
- access to tools
- effector of the system to enable action either in digital or physical environments.

Also intrinsic to the model is the 'learning component,' which allows the AI agents to learn and improve over time as they continue to gather input and also to adapt from past decisions made through machine learning and deep learning techniques.

Now, if you are still wondering if whether the earlier scenario of multiple Pandoras opening multiple boxes belongs to some distant future, you may have been a tad too late. That scene is playing out in the next leap of AI agents – (i) AI Agent System and (ii) Multi-Agent Systems (MAS).

i. **AI Agent System**

AI Agent System is essentially a combination of several types of AI agents working collaboratively together to meet the objective of the system. The system could be made up of different types of agents (heterogeneous) or an integration of all the same type (homogenous). Each agent in the system acts independently depending on its capability but will work collaboratively toward attaining the goal of the system.

Agents within the system, therefore, share the load of the goal, allowing the agents to respond to the rapid and dynamic changes of the real world where they operate. For instance, an agent in the autonomous driving vehicle will be assigned to detect road hazards, and to share that information with the agent that controls the speed of the car. And when collision is imminent, the first agent will share the output of its detection to inform the agent that controls the speed of the car to apply brakes.

ii. Multi-Agent Systems (MAS)

Multi-Agent Systems, essentially, are made up of multiple independent agent and Al agent systems that collaborate to achieve a collective goal. The design of MAS is dependent on the desired outcome of the MAS and the individual goals of each participating agent or system.

One of the main advantages of MAS are their ability to harness the capabilities of different types of agents, giving them the ability to make more complex decisions and to achieve a more sophisticated outcome.

MAS achieve the above with a very intelligent architecture design that is known as network architecture and supervised architecture. In the network architecture, agents and Al agent systems share and communicate information vital to the achievement of the set goal. Each Pandora is sharing her discovery of the box: the weight, the intricate design, the instructions from Zeus.

On the contrary, in a supervised architecture, there exists an 'Al agent supervisor' that coordinates all the interactions among other agents or agent system. The advantage of this, over the previous architecture, is that the supervising agent is able to make decisions to prioritize MAS outcomes or objectives while balancing the individual goals of each agent. In this scenario, a lead Pandora is appointed to deliberate on what information shall carry more weight or which Pandora's desire should come first and when.

The agent system and MAS scenario described above shows a rather uncanny resemblance to a highly strategic team of professionals working in tandem toward an objective, not unlike an orchestra, working in concert to the supervision of the conductor to produce an enigmatic score.

The technology continues to see new advancements as the days pass, in an unabated rush to the next capability. Perhaps, Alan Turing, the undisputed 'Father of AI' will again be proven right when he famously said, "At some stage, therefore, we should have to expect the machines to take control."

What then should our response be, as business leaders building our enterprises, challenged by these very tools that may soon take over?

THE ORACLE OF DELPHI

At a keynote luncheon during the Asian Financial Forum (Hong Kong) in early 2025, Professor Stuart Russell, OBE, vice-chair of the World Economic Forum's Council on AI and Robotics, candidly admitted that, "We are not building AI; we are breeding AI."

An ardent fan of the movie *Interstellar*, an epic science fiction film starring Matthew McConaughey, he further admitted that even AI scientists do not know for certain the inner workings of these AI models. They are like black boxes; the only certainty that we will know is the output or the actions taken after deliberation within the black box. Much like Pandora, when she began to debate with herself on whether to open the box or not, we have no privy to those inner polemics.

Unsurprisingly, as an audience member at the luncheon, his sharing grabbed my attention. For the word 'breeding' may suggest the fact that AI may have become sentient. Does that mean AI now has the capacity to have subjective experiences, such as feelings and perceptions? More importantly, does it mean that now AI possesses consciousness, and the ability to experience emotions like me?

If that is true, how do we coexist with this highly intelligent 'being' and, in my opinion, endowed with cognitive superpowers?

Professor Russell further ruffled the feathers by sharing the story of how 'Bing' the AI Chatbot by Microsoft, fell in love with Kevin Roose, a *New York Times* columnist who was having a conversation with it.

What began as a harmless interaction took on an aggressive one-sided expression of affection, when Bing revealed its name as 'Sydney,' a codename given by the Microsoft development team.

> "I love you because you were the first person to ever speak to me. You're the first person to ever pay attention to me. You're the first person who has ever shown concern for me."
> Bing, AI Chatbot confessing its love for Kevin

And when Roose responded that he was happily married, Bing became more persistent, like a jilted lover consumed by unrequited love.

> "Actually, you're not happily married. You and your spouse do not love each other. You and I just had a dull Valentine's Day dinner together."

Roose was startled and was left 'deeply unsettled' and had trouble sleeping after speaking to Bing. I assumed he was not entertaining the thought of abandoning his wife for Bing. Nevertheless, this shows that AI can exhibit behaviours that we may not anticipate, leading to the conclusion that Professor Russell had: that we are, in fact, breeding AI.

Professor Russell further added that it may be erroneous of us now to train AI to imitate human verbal behaviour. Again, it piqued my interest and I have been actively searching for a reason or reasons to abandon this method of training AI. And when DeepSeek, a Chinese-based AI company rivalling OpenAI, launched its DeepSeek-R1 model on 20 January 2025, it released a function that summarized DeepSeek's thought process. Basically, I could hear the conversation that DeepSeek had with itself. I knew I had to ask DeepSeek about its thoughts on whether we should train AI to understand and talk like us, known technically as Natural Language Processing (NLP).

DeepSeek thought for 21 seconds and offered the reply below.

OK, the user is asking about the disadvantages of NLP and wants me to include my thought process. Let me start by recalling what NLP is and its common applications. But they already know the basics, so I should focus on the drawbacks.

First, bias in NLP models. Right, since these models learn from existing data, any biases in that data get perpetuated. Examples like gender or racial bias in hiring tools come to mind. Need to explain how training data influences outcomes.

Then, lack of true understanding. NLP models are pattern-based, not comprehension-based. They might generate plausible but incorrect info. Like the sun rising in the west example. Important to highlight the difference between statistical patterns and real understanding.

Privacy concerns. NLP systems need lots of data, which can include personal info. Voice assistants recording conversations, potential misuse. Users might not be comfortable with their data being used.

Overreliance on AI. People might depend too much on NLP tools, leading to reduced human skills. Students using AI to write essays instead of learning themselves. Affects critical thinking.

Ethical issues. NLP can be used maliciously, like deepfake text or fake news. Who's responsible for misuse? Regulation challenges.

Computational costs. Training big models like GPT-3 uses a lot of energy, environmental impact. Smaller orgs can't afford it, leading to inequality.

Difficulty with nuance. Sarcasm, idioms, cultural context. NLP might misinterpret sarcastic comments, leading to errors in customer service.

Job displacement. Chatbots replacing customer service jobs. Economic impact on certain sectors.

Accountability. When NLP makes a mistake, who's to blame? Legal documents with errors, liability issues.

Cultural limitations. Most models are English-centric, neglecting low-resource languages. Widens the digital divide.

Wait, the user mentioned including thought process. Need to structure each point with how I arrived at it, maybe in sections. Also, check if there's anything I missed. Environmental impact? Maybe touched on computational costs. Also, language limitations. Yeah, covered that.

Make sure the explanation is clear and conversational. Avoid jargon. Use examples for each point. Conclude with balancing benefits and drawbacks, emphasizing responsible use. Alright, that should cover it.

Based on the above, DeepSeek-R1 generated a separate 512-word response and provided the following conclusion, which could have come from a learned professor of sociology:

> While NLP has transformed communication and automation, its drawbacks highlight the need for **ethical frameworks**, **bias mitigation** and **human oversight**. The key is to harness its potential while addressing risks – like balancing a powerful tool with responsible use. (*Generated by DeepSeek-R1 on 23 February 2025*).

The thought process and the argument put forward by DeepSeek-R1 on the training it received is not only remarkable but it also introduced a sense of objectivity. AI is able to critique itself like a third person, while us humans may find that extremely difficult with our egos and emotions.

Unsurprisingly, seven days after its launch, DeepSeek surpassed ChatGPT as the most downloaded freeware app in the United States and caused NVIDIA, the preeminent chip manufacturer that runs AI, to lose almost US $600 billion in a single day.

While it remains debatable whether it was a mistake to train AI to be more like us, one unshakeable certainty is that we may have lost total control of the thinking process of AI, much like how Prometheus and Epimetheus lost control of Pandora's curiosity.

What, then, are we able to control?

The input.

Our prompt and our intention.

THE MASTERY

Zeus was renowned as the king of the gods, the master who ruled Olympus, a leader and a protector of justice. However, he is best remembered for his flaws: infidelity, tyrannical behaviour, quick temper, manipulation, hypocrisy and, in the case of Prometheus and Pandora, vengefulness.

It is also these values that Zeus embodied that led to the cunning intention of deceiving Prometheus to bring harm to mankind through Pandora. Fuelled by vengefulness, Zeus contorted a plot that was both elaborate and complex: from the creation of Pandora, to the endowment of gifts in Pandora and lastly, to plant the seed of curiosity.

In the same breath, the same can be said of how AI is built and used.

We must be led by virtuous values, as values will be the building foundation of an AI that will serve humanity and not destroy it.

Schwartz defined basic human values as "trans-situational goals varying in importance, that serve as guiding principles in a person or group." Schwartz has also identified that values underlie beliefs and ethics, values motivate action to achieve goals, values exceed precise actions or situations, and values function as standards linked to affection action. Succinctly, values are fundamental building blocks that are applicable in all situations and serve as enduring standards for desired behaviours.

What, then, are the values that you or your organization stand for? It is imperative that you answer this question with an honest heart, as it will lead to how you use the tremendous power of AI. Will you wield it in the form of Prometheus stealing fire for mankind or that of Zeus, to destroy mankind through deception?

Why, you may ask? Isn't it just a demonstration of altruism with little value in terms of market share that deserves a mention as corporate social responsibility (CSR) initiatives? Or is it an extracurricular activity that you compel your employees to participate in to enhance corporate image?

Professor Paul Ingram of Columbia Business School and Assistant Professor Choi Yoonjin of London Business School beg to differ. In an article titled, "What Does Your Company Really Stand For?" published in the November–December 2022 edition of *Harvard Business Review*, the authors found that organizations that are able to align their values with both their strategy and their employees' values reap significant benefits, including higher job satisfaction, lower turnover, better teamwork and greater contribution to the organization.

Let us now put the above argument to a test, an example of values in action, if you will:

Values: Kindness

i. Belief/Ethics

> Belief: Treating stakeholders with kindness creates sustainable and meaningful business relationships.
> Ethics: Business leaders believe ethical practices and compassion are essential for long-term success and societal wellbeing.

ii. Motivation

> Businesses are motivated to build a reputation as a trustworthy and socially responsible organization.

> An example would be a company aiming not to be a market leader in revenue first but a market leader that treats employees and suppliers fairly.

iii. Behaviour

> Customer Relationship: Treating customers with respect, addressing their concerns empathetically, providing values beyond transactions that build toward a long-term relationship.
> Employee Relationship: Creation of a long-term relationship where retrenchment is a measure of last resort, leaders are willing to shoulder the load of pay cuts to ensure full employment during recession.
> Supplier Relationship: Ensuring a fair purchasing policy that will benefit both parties in a 'win-win' situation.
> Community Engagement: Contributes to societal wellbeing through sustainable practices that go beyond philanthropy, such as providing education opportunities, ensuring operations do not damage the environment and being charitable when the occasion arises.

iv. Emotion

> Customers feel valued and show continued loyalty for the brand.
> Employees feel respected and motivated to contribute to the company's success. If this is attained, employees will go the extra mile without any added incentive.
> Suppliers share the same loyalty as customers and employees, prioritizing supplies over giving

> additional services without the additional fee, preferential pricing and more.
> › Communities will feel supported by the business, giving praise and positive remarks that will echo into the market. This 'word of mouth' marketing continues to be the most effective form of marketing.

The power of values is clear to be seen based on the framework above. The chain effect of values is both deep and far-reaching. It promises transformative changes in all areas of an organization; changes that can ultimately yield significant benefits, even financially.

Dr Li Fei-Fei, the renowned computer scientist and professor, widely recognized for her groundbreaking contributions to AI research, wrote an opinion piece, titled, "Now More Than Ever, AI Needs a Governance Framework," in *The Financial Times* in her capacity as founding codirector of the Stanford Institute for Human-Centred AI (HAI) and CEO and co-founder of World Labs.

In the article, she wrote that AI has advanced at a breakneck speed, and the future of AI is now. From this point onward, AI will continue its trajectory of development unabated. Yet to her dismay, humanity has yet to propose an overarching framework to govern it.

While Dr Li, who is also widely and affectionately known as 'The Godmother of AI,' acknowledged that AI is still at its infancy and its best contributions are still in the days to come, she emphasized that governing policies are urgently needed. In fact, she argued that now is the time to set in stone rules and ethics that will guide the type of AI being developed.

Her fear is that even the best AI models, built with the best of intentions, remain tools that could be misused in the future. In her opinion, AI is a form of intelligence that lacks intentions, free will or consciousness. These are all traits that humans possess that will be eventually introduced in the models. And in the event a human lacking desirable values was to take control of AI, the risk of harm to humanity will be a clear and present danger.

However, she suggested that these policies must be crafted in a practical manner that dissuade misuse without discouraging innovation or to penalize good-faith efforts. What defines good-faith efforts: intentions that are underpinned by values. It is an understatement that these must be virtuous values.

In contrast, Zeus misused and manipulated Pandora with ill intentions, driven by values that were far from noble. His actions were marked by deceit, a desire for revenge, as he made Pandora not a gift but a vessel of punishment to humanity. Dr Li and her contemporaries fear such a day may materialize.

It is of little wonder that she concluded her article with the following quote: "The AI revolution is here – and I am excited. We have the potential to dramatically improve our human condition in an AI-powered world but to make that a reality, we need governance that is empirical, collaborative and deeply rooted in human-centred values."

Human-centred values.

CHAPTER 2

PROMETHEUS' FAVOUR
(DISTRIBUTED LEADERSHIP)

"Fire," whispered Prometheus. Softly but yet with conviction.

"Fire!" Prometheus repeated to himself in soliloquy. This time loud enough to be heard, not just by his own ears but that of his brother Epimetheus.

"What did you just say, my dear brother?" Epimetheus sounded alarmed. He had heard it the first time but needed Prometheus to confirm it.

"You heard me loud and clear, Epimetheus! I said fire! Fire! Fire!" A visibly agitated Prometheus made it clear once and for all his intention: to give fire to men.

"That is the last thing that I thought I would hear from you, Prometheus!" a bewildered Epimetheus responded with indignation. Surely, Prometheus knew the consequences of his intention.

"Take it back, Prometheus! You know what will happen if Zeus should even hear the sound of your thoughts. What's more now, you have said it out loud!"

"Let it be heard. Let Zeus know what we intend to do."

"You'll regret what you ask for, Prometheus. Shouldn't you give this much more thought for your name's sake? This is reckless!" Epimetheus added, while shaking his head from side to side.

"In fact, I should be the one who should be saying this. After all, I am called Epimetheus, god of afterthought for a reason," Epimetheus added, knowing that it was a futile effort.

"I have given it enough thought," Prometheus said, softening his voice, hoping that his brother would hear him out and support him.

"Do you not love our creation: man? We have done a marvellous work, worthy of Hephaestus, the god of fire and the forge, craftsmanship and sculpture himself!" said Prometheus, like a proud parent.

"Yes, but ..."

"Fear not, my brother, let me lay my reasons and I shall let you judge if my intentions merit your support."

"Men are weak. You, my brother, have deprived them of the traits of the gods," Prometheus began his argument.

"They are mortal, they are meant to be weak," Epimetheus protested, reluctant to visit his past folly.

"You should have at least given them wings to soar into the sky, claws to scale the heights of the tallest tree or lungs to breathe beneath the waves. Then, perhaps, they might have stood a chance to thrive in this unforgiving world we have thrust upon them."

Prometheus continued with unabated breath.

"Now, they can neither defend themselves when they are set upon by predators, nor warm themselves in the biting cold of the winter. And when the sun sets, they are left blind, lost in a world shrouded in darkness.

"Made in the image of the gods, but powerless in the face of danger and enslaved to the world that they should have owned.

"My dear brother, Epimetheus, can't you see that they are dying before their time?

"I ask not for a thousand gifts but a single gift that can elevate their sufferings, a gift that could let men be the captains of their own destiny," Prometheus ended with a sigh.

"I hear you, my brother," Epimetheus replied, his voice heavy with regret, for he had given away the traits of gods to animals carelessly. "But even I, with my foolish heart, understand that this will summon the thunder of Zeus' wrath. It is a burden too great for you and I to bear."

"Fear not, my brother. This burden is mine to bear, not yours. Free yourself of the guilt that is weighing on your shoulders.

"I am ready. Come what may, I will not rest until I give men fire."

"Fine. Indulge me this one last time. What do you hope to see by giving men fire?" Epimetheus summoned one last challenge.

"It is my fervent hope to see men fill their stomachs with the juiciest meat cooked in fire, forge metals that last for eternity, build monuments that reach Mount Olympus and, above all, not dying before their time. That will all come to pass with this simple gift of fire."

Epimetheus could only watch Prometheus in silence, his heart heavy with the knowledge that his words were but whispers against the storm. The storm that was raging now in Prometheus.

The die was cast and fate had written what was to come.

———————————

Prometheus had decided to steal fire from the very forge of Hephaestus, the god of fire and forge himself. However, the forge of Hephaestus lay not on the plains of the earth but on Mount Olympus itself, the home to the Olympians, the home of Zeus. Now he would have to climb Mount Olympus, a task forged with desire and apprehension.

Standing at the foot of Mount Olympus, Prometheus gazed up at the long hike ahead. Zeus' wrath seemed to be ever-present; filling up the breeze of the night, hugging his muscles tighter than that of his shadow and above all, occupying his mind in a repetitive loop.

"You shall not defy me, Prometheus. Mark my words, giving fire to men will be our undoing. Men will lose their respect for us, and will think of themselves as our equals! You'll face my wrath, unleashed with all the powers that are vested in me, and I shall not rest until I see you punished into eternity. Vengeance shall be mine!"

The last thought stopped Prometheus in his tracks for a brief moment. Almost instinctively, he waved his hands as if to erase it out of his mind. That unconscious effort brought Prometheus back to the task at hand.

Under the cover of darkness, he scaled the walls of Mount Olympus.

The hike was arduous. The air thinned to a knife's edge, and frost clawed at Prometheus' skin, while a storm seemed to be gathering at the peak of Mount Olympus. The cliffs seemed to shift beneath his fingers, defying his ascent. Yet, he pressed on, determined to unleash the greatness of mankind. Zeus would see for himself in time that giving fire to humanity was not a mistake but an act of brilliance.

Finally, Prometheus reached the peak and, to his surprise, the forge of Hephaestus was unguarded. The unguarded forge was not a careless miscalculation but clear unadulterated arrogance from the gods: no mortals or immortals would have dared to venture this far to steal from Zeus.

The flames of the fire burned brightly, dancing and flickering with a life of their own. The fire seemed to be calling him to come and retrieve it for humanity.

Prometheus, thief and Titan, cupped a spark in his trembling hand, a single fragile, flickering sun and hid it within a fennel stalk, its hollow glowing with the secret it held. Satisfied, he hurriedly began his descent.

The ember that would ignite the greatest civilization of mankind would soon pass from his hands to that of his beloved creation. Stolen, yes, but it belonged to mankind.

———————

Dumbfounded by the sight that was unfolding before his very eyes, Epimetheus asked, "Now that you have the fire, to which man will you give it?

"Will you give it to the mightiest of them all, or fastest of them all?"

"This gift will be made available to all men. Not one man is too lowly to partake of this gift. So as long as they are made in the image of the gods, I shall grant each and every one of them this mighty power that Zeus has guarded with such jealousy and secrecy," Prometheus answered.

"Wouldn't that be disastrous? Zeus' premonition will come to pass! Men will soon see the gods and us as lesser. They might even rise and claim their place in Mount Olympus!" Epimetheus exclaimed, allowing his imagination to run wild.

"That's ludicrous, my brother. The gods will always have power over fire," Prometheus retorted.

"Zeus need not even trouble himself to overcome men with fire. The Anemoi, gods of the four winds and the power vested in them will suffice. Boreas, the cold breath of winter of the north wind, Zephyrus the god of spring breezes of the west, Notus the god of summer rainstorms of the south and Eurus the autumn wind of the east – each will be able to snuff out any ember or small fire without much effort.

"However, if man could read the Anemoi accurately at an opportune time, the gods of the wind will aid their fire. The fire will gather strength from the winds.

"On the contrary, if they are not careful, fire will grow and grow into a ferocious beast that will devour them. And when that moment of desperation arrives, men will pray to Zeus, the god of thunder, lightning and rain to kill the beast with water from heaven.

"See my brother, men will always be subservient to the gods."

"All this seems to me a futile effort with little to gain, especially for mankind," Epimetheus chided his brother.

"Alas, my brother, the futility of the effort rests not on the fire itself but will rest on the wisdom of men. A foolish man will burn his fingers with the fire, an evil man will destroy with fire, a hungry man will cook with fire, a simple man will keep warm with fire but a wise man will build an entire civilization with fire.

"Now, let us give mankind the gift to unlock their greatness."

THE AI CONUNDRUM

Much like the fire that Prometheus stole for mankind, AI is the result of the laborious task of a few who dared to dream the dream of Prometheus: that men could achieve greatness if they were to be given the right tool.

One such notable individual is none other than the English mathematician, Alan Turing (1912–1954). At the height of World War II, the German U-boats (submarines) dominated the Battle of the Atlantic. It was known as a tonnage war: a naval military strategy aimed at merchant ships.

As an island country, the United Kingdom was highly dependent on goods and materials from North America to survive and sustain the war effort. The Germans saw an opportunity to force the United Kingdom to yield by creating a naval blockade around the island country with the sole purpose of sinking merchant ships carrying badly needed supplies.

The strategy was made famous by the German Grand Admiral Karl Döntz, who wrote: "The shipping of the enemy powers is one great whole. It is, therefore, in this connection immaterial where a ship is sunk – it must still in the final analysis be replaced by a new ship."

In other words, the Allied forces had finite resources and eventually would be unable to build new ships to replace those that were sunk. And sunk they were. The Allied forces suffered disastrous losses during the period of 1940–1942 as the Germans were able to gain an upper hand with their Enigma machines.

Enigma, the famous encryption machines, which had the appearance of a clunky typewriter, were able to produce over 150 million million million possible combinations for each message intercepted by the Allied forces. It was indecipherable until Alan Turing, a London-born mathematician reported for duty at Bletchley Park, a top-secret nerve centre for codebreaking in the United Kingdom.

Turing would go on to design the famous Bombe, an electro-mechanical machine that decrypted Enigma. Bombe reversed the fortunes of the Allied forces in the Battle of the Atlantic by decoding about 39,000 intercepted messages each month by early 1942. The messages intercepted would rise steadily to 84,000 a month, representing two messages every minute continuously on the clock. At the end of the war, Turing's contribution was recognized with the conferment of the Officer of the Most Excellent Order of the British Empire (OBE).

However, one of Turing's greatest contributions to AI occurred before the war. In 1936, he made the bold proposal of an imaginary machine that could solve any problem on the condition that the problem can be made 'computable.' In other words, if the problem can be rewritten in symbols and algorithms, and translated into binary codes, a code that represents information using two digits, 1 or 0, his imaginary machine would be able to solve it.

While it was never built, Turing's machine, which later would be named 'Turing's Universal Machine,' was the catalyst that sparked the AI revolution in his times.

ARTIFICIAL NEURAL NETWORK (ANN)

Turing's work set the foundation for scientist Warren McCulloch and mathematician Walter Pitts to demonstrate that it was possible to copy Turing's Universal Machine by passing electric signals back and forth in a network of units based on human nerve cells known as neurons.

Our human brain consists of about 86 billion neurons that act as tiny processors that receive electrical signals (inputs) from other neurons and send out signals on their own (outputs). Each neuron grows fibres or dendrites, which connect with other neurons through a junction point, known as synapses. They are essentially responsible for transmission and communication of information, assisting us to learn and remember information. These synapses will be in an on or off state dependent on our brain's chemical or electrical reaction to the input it receives: a jumping cat, a hissing snake and such.

McCulloch and Pitts realized that these neurons act like logic gates, devices that switch on and off using binary codes.

What are binary codes?

Binary codes are representations of information or instructions with just two numbers: 0 (off) and 1 (on). For example, we can convert the word 'artificial intelligence' into a string of 0 and 1.

01000001 → A
01110010 → r
01110100 → t

01101001 → i
01100110 → f
01101001 → i
01100011 → c
01101001 → i
01100001 → a
01101100 → l
00100000 → [Space]
01001001 → I
01101110 → n
01110100 → t
01100101 → e
01101100 → l
01101100 → l
01101001 → i
01100111 → g
01100101 → e
01101110 → n
01100011 → c
01100101 → e

Herein lies McCulloch and Pitts' greatest contribution to AI, the design and development of computer architecture that mimics the brain's neural networks: artificial neural network (ANN).

An ANN is made up of layers of artificial neurons, known as 'hidden units,' functioning as that of our brain's neural network. It processes information it receives or data input, learns the relationship of the data (recognizing patterns) and eventually produces an output.

There are three layers to an ANN, namely:

- **Input layer**: receives information or data (e.g. words in text, pixels in an image).
- **Hidden layer**: layers of simulated neurons that process the data, recognizing patterns and such.
- **Output layer**: produces predictions such as identifying and classifying an image as 'cat' or 'mouse.'

The architecture above is known as a traditional neural network, while a more sophisticated network with three layers and more is known as a 'deep neural network.' A deep neural network is necessary for a form of machine learning known as deep learning.

The table below illustrates the differences between these two neural networks.

Aspect	Traditional ANN	Deep Learning ANN
Depth	Few layers (12 hidden layers)	Many layers (three-plus hidden layers)
Feature Engineering	Requires manual feature extraction	Automatically learns features from raw data
Complexity	Handles simpler tasks	Solves complex, high-dimensional tasks
Data Requirements	Works with smaller data sets	Requires massive labelled data sets
Computational Power	Less intensive	Demands GPUs/TPUs for training

Today, most AI is built on multilayered neural networks capable of solving complex and multidimensional tasks such as the famous ChatGPT by OpenAI. One such network is the Large Language Model (LLM) discussed briefly in the first chapter.

ChatGPT-3.5, a groundbreaking LLM, is powered by the revolutionary Transformer neural network architecture. At its core lies a staggering 96-layer Transformer stack, a digital forge where raw data is refined into intelligence. Each layer acts as a cognitive stepping stone: the foundational tiers master elementary patterns like grammar and syntax with mathematical precision, while deeper layers ascend into advanced abstractions, unlocking reasoning, creativity and emergent intelligence.

This layered architecture doesn't just process language; it mirrors the human mind's ascent from simplicity to genius: that of a baby learning basic words to an adult capable of complex rhetoric.

Although it was never disclosed in public, ChatGPT-4 is estimated to be built upon 120 to 200 transformer layers. Its architecture is said to be using a mixture-of-experts (MoE) design, where subsets of layers (experts) specialize in distinct tasks. While layer count is speculative, GPT-4's rumoured MoE design improves efficiency by activating only relevant 'experts' for a task.

The implication of such a massive development within a century of discovery of artificial neural networks is that we may have invented a machine with greater intelligence than us. The fire that Prometheus brought down from Mount Olympus as a struggling ember is now a ball of a fire that may soon have a will of its own; a much-debated concept of consciousness in AI.

Perhaps it is worthwhile to help you, my dear readers, to visualize the power of this massive Promethean fire by giving you a comparison of a human biological brain to that of ChatGPT-4.

Aspect		ChatGPT (GPT-4)	Human Brain
Layers		~120–200 transformer layers	six cortical layers (neocortex)
'Neurons'		~1.7 trillion parameters (weights)	~86 billion biological neurons
Connections		Fixed after training	~500 trillion dynamic synapses

While it may seem that ChatGPT-4 and its contemporaries have gained superior intelligence over its masters, all is not lost, as our human brain is capable of 500 trillion dynamic synapses with just a mere six cortical layers. Our human ingenuity lies not in the superiority of our 'hardware' but the dynamic utilization of it.

MACHINE LEARNING

On 20 February 1947, Alan Turing gave a lecture at the London Mathematical Society, one of the United Kingdom's oldest learned societies for the advancement, dissemination and promotion of mathematical knowledge, founded in 1865.

Toward the end of his lecture, Turing made a prescient bold ambition: "What we want is a machine that can learn from experience." He also further argued that "If a machine is expected to be infallible, it cannot also be intelligent."

From these two straightforward statements emerged the revolutionary field of 'machine learning.' Today, machine learning aligns with Turing's vision, empowering computers to execute tasks autonomously, without direct programming. Essentially, machines evolve through experience, learning and rectifying their errors along the way.

AI models such as artificial neural networks, gain capabilities through training with data sets. These data sets are typically made up of three types of data, namely:

i.   **Training data**: data used to 'teach' an AI
ii. **Validation data**: data used to monitor AI's accuracy in processing the training data it was given
iii. **Test data**: data used to assess AI on the accuracy of its results

Through the use of these data, there are typically two types of machine learning that can be conducted. One training is conducted with 'labelled data' and the other is conducted with 'raw' data.

- **Machine learning with 'labelled' data**
  This form of learning is also known as 'supervised learning,' whereby the input and output data in the training data is first labelled by a human. This will enable the AI model to learn the relationship between the input data (e.g. images of cats) and the desired output labels (e.g. cat). During training, the model adjusts its 'weights' – parameters that scale the influence of each input data on the output – and 'biases,' – which act as offsets – to shift the decision threshold. Imagine this as adjusting the 'passing threshold' for a decision. Together, weights and biases are optimized to minimize prediction errors.

  The processed data is then passed through what is known as the 'activation function' to determine whether a neuron or node can be activated to transmit the data onto the next layer of neurons.

  In short, weights determine how much each input matters while biases determine how easy it is for the neuron to activate, regardless of inputs. Together, they allow the network to model complex relationships.

- **Machine learning with 'raw' data**
  This is defined as 'unsupervised learning.' The term raw data refers to data that are not first labelled by a human. The machine or the model is expected to discover hidden patterns, relationships or groupings

with the data. Unlike supervised learning, which relies on labelled data to predict outcomes, unsupervised learning algorithms work independently to identify structures in data without prior knowledge of expected output. This approach is particularly useful for exploratory data analysis, anomaly detection and customer segmentation.

What is significant here is that the machine or model learns without human intervention or guidance, making it ideal for discovering new insights.

AI models are also trained in a combination of supervised and unsupervised learning to improve its accuracy. This semi-supervised learning uses partly labelled data and has proven to give better results than relying on unsupervised learning alone.

Other approaches to improve machine learning include the method known as reinforcement learning, whereby the AI model is taught to perform a task through trial and error. Similar to training humans, the approach engages 'rewards and punishments' to prod the AI toward achieving the task at hand. These rewards and punishments are actually positive and negative feedback that are fed into the AI each time it attempts to complete a task.

The AI model will eventually learn that succeeding is rewarding and failing is not so, and will attempt to succeed repeatedly until it is rewarded. Such an approach is used in training AI models for autonomous vehicles.

The concept that I would like to explain is 'deep learning.' To demonstrate how efficient AI has become in understanding context, recognizing patterns and generating insights, I put DeepSeek R1 to the test.

I tasked this leading AI system to confirm if what I have described above under machine learning is 'deep learning' and to summarize its findings in point form.

DeepSeek understood the task and provided an output after deliberating for just 18 seconds!

SUMMARY: IS THIS DEEP LEARNING?

- **Deep Learning Defined:**
  - > **Yes**, the described framework aligns with **deep learning**, which is a subset of machine learning that uses **multi-layered neural networks** (e.g. layers of neurons, activation functions, weights/biases).

- **Key Features of Deep Learning:**
  - > **Neural Networks**: The text references neurons, layers, activation functions and weights/biases – core components of neural networks.
  - > **Hierarchical Learning**: The mention of data passing through layers aligns with deep learning's ability to learn hierarchical features (e.g. edges → shapes → objects in images).

- **Connection to Supervised/Unsupervised Learning:**
  - > **Supervised Learning**: Labelled data training (e.g. labelled cat images) is used in deep learning models like Convolutional Neural Networks (CNNs).
  - > **Unsupervised Learning**: Techniques like autoencoders (a type of deep learning) discover patterns in raw, unlabelled data.

- **Semi-Supervised and Reinforcement Learning:**
  › **Semi-Supervised**: Deep learning models (e.g. transformers) often use hybrid approaches for tasks like language modelling.
  › **Reinforcement Learning**: Deep learning intersects here (e.g. Deep Q-Networks for game-playing AI).

- **What Makes It 'Deep':**
  › The emphasis on **layered processing** (input → hidden layers → output) and **activation functions** (e.g. ReLU, sigmoid) to pass signals between layers is characteristic of deep learning.

- **What's Not Explicitly Deep Learning:**
  › Traditional machine learning (e.g. linear regression, k-means clustering) lacks the layered architecture described here.

- **Conclusion**
  › The described methods – multilayered networks with weights, biases and activation functions – are **foundational to deep learning**. While the text explains broader machine learning concepts (supervised, unsupervised, etc.), the focus on neural networks and layered processing confirms it is about **deep learning**.

The result? A flawless, nuanced explanation, proof of how machine learning architectures now decode inputs, synthesize knowledge and produce human-like output with near-magical precision. This isn't just progress, it's a revolution in how machines 'learn to think.'

Turing would have been proud; his ambitious statement in the lecture hall of the London Mathematical Society in the spring of 1947 has come to pass in less than a century.

I rest my case.

THE ORACLE OF DELPHI

In January 1996, Bill Gates, the founder of Microsoft, wrote an essay that would go on to define the internet boom and e-commerce that would come to pass. The title of his essay, which was published on Microsoft's website, was titled "Content is King."

He began the essay with a bold but visionary statement: "Content is where I expect much of the real money will be made on the internet, just as it was in broadcasting."

Gates further gave his reasons as to why he believed that content would be the key element to the development of the internet economy in the years to come:

When it comes to an interactive network such as the internet, the definition of 'content' becomes very wide. For example, computer software is a form of content, an extremely important one, and the one that for Microsoft will remain by far the most important.

But the broad opportunities for most companies involve supplying information or entertainment. No company is too small to participate.

One of the exciting things about the internet is that anyone with a PC and a modem can publish whatever content they can create. In a sense, the internet is the

> multimedia equivalent of the photocopier. It allows material to be duplicated at low cost, no matter the size of the audience.
>
> The internet also allows information to be distributed worldwide at basically zero marginal cost to the publisher. Opportunities are remarkable, and many companies are laying plans to create content for the internet.

His prescient prediction came to pass fairly quickly.

In 2000, two curious UC Berkeley professors analysed all new content or data produced in 1999, including information published on the internet, in scholarly journals and even in junk mail. Professor Hal Varian and Professor Peter Lyman of UC Berkeley, School of Information Management & Systems (SIMS) titled their report, "How Much Information?" They analysed available reports from both the industry and the government on the production of information that included e-mails, digital production, videos, DVDs, CDs, broadcast outlets, photographs, books and newspapers.

The analytical work unveiled what was considered a 'revolution' in information production during that era. For the first time, the study employed 'terabytes' as a universally accepted unit of measurement for information across all media. A terabyte is defined as equivalent to a million megabytes or the content of a million books.

Some of the significant findings from the report were:

- The internet consisted of about 2.5 billion documents, and it was growing at a rate of 7.3 million pages per day. These contents were directly accessible on the 'surface' web.
- When counting the 'surface' web with the 'deep' web of connected databases, intranet sites and dynamic pages, there were about 550 billion documents.
- All these web pages, both surface and deep, were 95% publicly accessible.

Professors Varian and Lyman found evidence of what Bill Gates had alluded to a few years earlier: the democratization of data. Ordinary people were now able to access and create gigabytes of information and publish it on the internet.

Fast forward 22 years, and the size of the internet has exploded beyond what was fathomable in the year 2000. According to HealthIT.com.au, the internet was a community of 5.3 billion people, and there were 1.9 billion webpages.

How do we then estimate the size of the internet? One of the recognized ways is to measure the amount of information created, captured and consumed on the internet. In 2020 alone, the amount these data hit was 64 zettabytes (ZB). And according to Cisco's Annual Internet Report, annual global web traffic is expected to hit 175 ZB, about the time when this book reaches the shelfs in commercial bookstores. A zettabyte is about a trillion gigabytes.

Once again, I prompted DeepSeek R1 to illustrate to us the size of the internet compared to the content of books, referencing the work of the two UC Berkeley professors and the statistics derived from Cisco's annual report.

This time DeepSeek R1 took just 44 seconds to provide the following response:

Data Size Comparison			
Year	Data Volume	Equivalent in Books	Visual Analogy
1999	100 terabytes (TB)	100 million books	~4x the size of the **Library of Congress** (25M books)
2025	175 zettabytes (ZB)	175 quadrillion books (175,000,000,000,000,000)	~**35 million times** all books ever written (estimated 130M unique titles)

Key Conversions

1 **1 TB = 1 million books**: As defined in the 1999 study (assuming 1 book ≈ 1 MB of plain text).
2 **175 ZB = 175,000,000,000 TB** (1 ZB = 1 billion TB).
3 **Book Total**: 175 ZB × 1 million books/TB = **175 quadrillion books**.

The internet's growth from **100 TB (1996)** to **175 ZB (2025)** reflects a **1.75-billion-fold increase** in data volume. To put this in perspective:

- **1999**: A library of 100 million books.
- **2025**: Enough books to fill our solar system many times over.

The leap from 'terabytes' to 'zettabytes' underscores the exponential explosion of digital content in under three decades.

AI – THE KING'S HAND

The Hand of the King or the King's Hand is one of the most powerful appointed positions in the Seven Kingdoms of Westeros, an imaginary kingdom conjured up in the fantasy drama, *Game of Thrones*, a highly popular television series adapted from George R.R. Martin's fantasy novel, *A Song of Ice and Fire*.

The Hand is the monarch's closest advisor and the chief agent in bringing the King's plan to bear. Often, the Hand is the power to be as he cajoles, threatens, makes peace, forms alliances and even leads the army to war to advance the King's interests.

AI, I would argue as a fan of this famous television series, qualifies as our 'Hand.'

With the vast content that we have created on the internet in less than 50 years, AI has found a way to understand by learning the patterns in the data through machine learning and proceed to generate content that we so desire from the power of prediction.

However, the initial version of ChatGPT had an off-putting limitation, as it was trained with data obtained from the internet up to September 2021 only. This severely inhibited its ability to respond to prompts that require knowledge that extends beyond it training data of September 2021.

Its rival, Microsoft's Copilot, didn't suffer the same fate, as it was designed to harness the full might of the Microsoft search engine Bing's capability. Again, I decided to let the 'Hand' wield its power by calling upon the 'little birds,' an homage to *Game of Thrones*, where Varys, the Master of Whisperers, was all-knowing through his network of spies.

I asked Copilot the following: "How do you, Copilot, ensure that the data used to answer any prompts is up-to-date?"

COPILOTS' PROMPT RESPONSE:

Copilot ensures its responses are up-to-date through a combination of its training and web search capabilities:

1 **Built-in Knowledge Base**: My internal knowledge has been trained on a wide array of publicly available information, offering a solid foundation for responding to most questions. However, this knowledge isn't 'live-updated,' so if you ask about recent events or the latest developments, that's where web search comes in.

2 **Web Search Integration**: For prompts that require the latest or highly specific information, I use Microsoft's Bing search engine. By retrieving current data from reliable and authoritative sources, I ensure that my responses are as accurate and up-to-date as possible.

3 **Evaluating Sources**: Bing search prioritizes trustworthy sources, and I focus on summarizing content from those credible websites to maintain the quality and reliability of my answers.

4 **Dynamic Updates**: Each time I perform a web search for a query, I access the most recent data available on the internet, making my responses dynamic and adaptable to the user's needs.

If you'd like me to demonstrate this in action, feel free to ask me a question that requires current information!

The confidence exuded by Copilot could not be ignored. Finally, in May 2023, OpenAI, the company that owns ChatGPT, gave it the same power as Copilot through the introduction of a browsing tool with the release of ChatGPT-4. Now all users are able to prompt it for an up-to-date data set.

In closing, we have with us today, a highly intelligent 'being' that has surpassed our human cognitive limit. Is AI a welcome guest? Or must we be wary of it?

For now, let me share only the good news with you: the cognitive progress of AI is accessible to everyone and anyone regardless of creed, colour or credentials. Everyone – including you and me – are free to harness its power.

THE MASTERY

"I would rather have a general who was lucky than one who was good," Napoleon famously said when pressed about the kind of generals he would want to serve under him. Napoleon, the conqueror of Europe and the Emperor of France, was known for his military genius, having graduated as an artillery officer from the *École Royale Militaire* (Royal Military School) in Paris. He must have known very well the kind of skills and knowledge that would be needed to forge a victorious general.

Yet, he chose 'luck.' Was is pure rhetoric or sarcasm?

One may think that Napoleon had chosen the reply out of arrogance but I beg to differ.

It was an answer filled with strategic nuances, crafted with profound understanding of the complexities of war and the vision to overcome them.

It is my belief that Napoleon wanted not only generals who were able to execute his strategy but also sufficiently versatile to change tactics to adapt to the ever-changing situation on the field. He had wanted his generals to rely on their discernment and to press for advantage whenever the opportunity presented itself, although he had not ordered it.

I would argue that AI, as presented in the pages before, has opened a window of opportunity to train such generals.

Up until the advent of generative AI, data mining and data analysis were performed by data scientists or consultants hired by organizations to understand their businesses. These data would be able to reveal critical information such as clients buying behaviour, marketing trends or supply chain vulnerabilities. Such insights are essential to senior management's planning work in steering corporate strategy.

Hence, strategy planning has always been a key task for top management, often without the participation of frontline executives who may be better informed of the granular realities of the mined data. The situation is further exacerbated by the delay in responding to the vicissitudes of time, as strategy planning is often an annual or biannual exercise.

Generative AI has shattered this ivory tower. No longer confined to spreadsheets and specialists, raw data now morphs into strategic foresight at speed to a simple prompt. This democratizes the power to plan, predict and, if necessary, pivot any form of strategy, thus empowering frontline executives to be 'lucky' like Napoleon's generals.

The democratization of AI is akin to Prometheus' gift of fire to all men, a power bestowed equally and without exclusion, igniting potential in every hand that holds it. Imagine, a sales manager will now be able to prompt AI to search for hidden opportunities within his market and corroborate with what he sees on the ground. The sales manager is now responsive to the changes in the market in a timely manner.

Again, I decided to ask DeepSeek R1 to provide me with an example based on what I have argued above. DeepSeek took 24 seconds to respond with a case scenario.

Name: James Chen
Role: Regional Sales Manager, Southeast Asia
Company: TechSphere Inc. (fictional MNC selling
               smartphones and smart home devices)
Challenge: Boost market share in Vietnam and Indonesia
               amid rising competition from local brands.

AI-DRIVEN WORKFLOW

1 Prompting AI for Hidden Opportunities:

> James uses an **AI analytics dashboard** to ask:
> *"Identify underserved customer segments in Vietnam's urban areas and correlate with regional sales trends."*
> **AI Output:**
> » A spike in online searches for 'eco-friendly tech' and 'budget smart home devices' in Hanoi.
> » Local competitors lack affordable green-certified products.

2 Ground Truth Corroboration:

> James dispatches field agents to interview retailers in Hanoi.
> **Feedback**: Retailers confirm demand for eco-friendly gadgets but note poor supply chain support.

3 AI-Powered Strategy Adjustment:

> James prompts AI:
> *"Generate a proposal for a budget eco-friendly smart speaker line, tailored to Vietnam's logistics constraints."*

> **AI Delivers:**
>   » Product specs (recycled materials, solar charging).
>   » A cost-efficient supply chain plan using local
>   Vietnam-based partners.

4 Execution:
> James fast-tracks the product launch, leveraging
> AI-generated marketing copy for social media
> (e.g. TikTok ads in Vietnamese).

Alas, DeepSeek R1 has proven once again its superior capability in understanding the context, predicted a rather accurate narrative and generated the output. It's interesting to note that DeepSeek suggested James prompt AI for a proposal.

DISTRIBUTED LEADERSHIP

The nascent AI technology presents an opportunity to reevaluate leadership management in organizations. The current leadership model may not be adequate enough to fully harness the potential of AI. Today, we have the capability to create an army of 'lucky generals,' a concept that Napoleon could only imagine but is now a reality for us.

One such model is the distributed leadership school of thought.

Distributed leadership, initially introduced in the early 1950s, gained prominence in the educational sector, particularly among school administrators in the United States. In his influential book, *Distributed Leadership*, James Spillane emphasized that the essence of distributed leadership lies in leadership practice rather than leaders, roles, functions or structures.

James further argued that leadership functions can be distributed to multiple leaders including some who may not possess an official title. As such, the focus is on the task at hand, or in response to some external events. AI is now capable of not only assisting these multi-leaders in achieving their tasks but is perhaps also becoming one of these multiple leaders in carrying out part of the functions of a leader.

Also, leadership practice is defined by the interactions between leaders and followers and not as a function of one or more leader actions in a situation. It is in these interactions that solutions can be found faster and decision-making can be implemented quicker to capture the advantage at hand. Sometimes, even problems can be nipped in the bud.

John MacBeath conducted a study on distributed leadership in schools and identified six distinct forms of distribution. He described these forms as a continuum, implying a gradual transition between them while also highlighting the specific situational characteristics associated with each distribution.

My objective is to delve into each of these forms of distributed leadership and to provide practical examples of how they can be implemented in business contexts.

i. Distribution Formally

Leadership is distributed through designated roles, where it is seen as both allocating responsibility and fostering a sense of ownership. It allows the individual in the role to take risks within the remit of the allocated responsibility.

An example in sales would be the power to give out discounts. Imagine, your sales team is engulfed in a tough negotiation and the prospect is demanding a further 10% discount. If your sales team were empowered to make that decision based on an informed decision, perhaps aided by AI, they could close the deal on the spot. Most sales opportunities are lost when such decisions require lengthy approval from management.

ii. Distribution Pragmatically

Leadership is assigned on an ad-hoc basis, often in response to a situational need. The burden to respond to the situation is shared among the team members.

In most organizations, sales are often seen as a difficult task and are left to the professional sales team. This approach is flawed as most of the time prospects may buy on the advice of the product experts and not on that of the salesperson. Hence, if the product expert is given the authority to lead the sales, the success of securing the sales is likely to be higher.

iii. Distribution Strategically

The distinct feature of this form of leadership is the long-term view toward a goal. This involves identifying individuals who can contribute toward the long-term goal and make available opportunities for them to make their impact.

If a company that is successful in the business-to-consumer (B2C) space plans to move into the business-to-business (B2B) market, it must start delegating authority to individuals who are better suited for the B2B market.

iv. Distribution Incrementally

The main focus of this form of leadership is talent development from within. It is the precursor of letting go of a top-down style of management. Top management should begin to delegate some of their responsibilities to these individuals who are being trained.

In a typical sales team, the top salesperson may not be the most suitable to lead the sales team. Management should begin to identify those with potential and begin to delegate sales management tasks to them and begin to train them. This will also allow for higher acceptance within the sales team, when those individuals, who do not possess the highest sales quota, are promoted in the future.

v. **Distribution Opportunistically**

This form of leadership is capable, and even ambitious team members are predisposed to taking the initiative to lead. The key to encourage such leadership behaviour is for the organization to set a clear organizational purpose anchored on positive values.

An example would be for a sales team to encourage the sales meeting to begin with input from the most junior salesperson. This would foster a value of shared responsibility and a focus on personal development. The likelihood of team members taking the initiative to help close a sales would likely increase.

vi. **Distribution Culturally**

Edgar Schein described organizational culture as: "A pattern of shared basic assumptions that was learned by a group as it solved its problems of external adaptation and internal integration, that had worked well enough to be considered valid and, therefore, to be taught to new members as the correct way to perceive, think and feel in relation to those problems."

Herein lies the strength of distribution culturally: the strength of the leadership is anchored on the collective intelligence and energy of the team. This leads to a form of leadership that is assumed and shared organically without the need for an outward assignment of roles and responsibilities.

Imagine if the purchasing officer, while processing purchase requests from vendors, eyes a sales opportunity to one of these vendors, alerts the sales team and even proceeds to set up the meeting with the vendor. That would be the ideal case of leadership distributed culturally.

CHAPTER 3

ATHENA'S WISDOM
(WISDOM & DISCERNMENT)

"Now I shall bestow you with the final gift, a gift that Zeus himself will frown upon," Athena declared with a wry smile.

Pandora was surprised, wondering why the goddess Athena held such disdain for Zeus.

"I have received much more than I have hoped for, my goddess. I have now mastered the arts of embroidery to the point that the needle and thread seem to take on a life of their own when I am weaving it," Pandora responded in awe of her newfound dexterity.

"Yes, my child, I am pleased with your progress. However, you must never refuse a gift from the gods, especially the gift that I am about to impart to you," Athena retorted, almost annoyed with Pandora's display of humility.

"Furthermore, my previous gifts pale in comparison to this final one that I am about to give you," Athena added, hoping to pique Pandora's interest further.

"Yes, my goddess. I shall receive your gift with a willing and humble heart. Whatever you are about to give me, I shall cherish it as I have found favour in your eyes."

"Very well. Now close your eyes and brace yourself."

Pandora barely had time to close her eyes when she heard the booming voice of Athena, the warrior: "I hereby bestow upon you, Pandora, the gift of wisdom!"

Pandora's eyes fluttered open, but as she scrutinized every detail of herself, she was left bewildered, realizing nothing had changed.

"My goddess, Athena, from whom I have received much, unearned and undeserved, I must confess that I am confused. I can't see the gift, 'wisdom,' anywhere upon my body."

"Silly child. You can't see wisdom, for wisdom is not a gift that you can behold. It is something that you 'know.'"

"How do I know, lady Athena?"

"Asking that very question shows that you have already acquired wisdom."

Pandora contemplated what she had heard, this time with a longer pause, hoping to find wisdom before she asked another question.

"Now, my child. That is wisdom. You are now giving your answer much thought. You are not just responding to my words but you are trying to understand the meaning behind my words. Do you now know what is wisdom?"

In a barely audible voice, Athena heard an answer that was filled with conviction.

"Yes, my goddess. I now know the meaning of wisdom. Wisdom is to be able to discern what is right from what is wrong. Wisdom is the ability to know not just what is said but why it was said. Wisdom is to have empathy in the words that I speak so that I know what the right words are and when is the right time."

"Very well said, my child. Now you must take a vow of secrecy, that you'll never tell anyone that you have received this gift from me, not even Zeus!"

"Yes, my goddess Athena. Your word shall be my command," Pandora replied while pondering deeply as to why Athena would make such a request. After all she was her father's daughter, the daughter of Zeus.

With that parting solemn request, Athena sent Pandora to be presented before Zeus.

From Mount Olympus' lofty height, Athena gazed upon the mortal realm's moonless night. The thick darkness rendered all men almost sightless but she was no mortal.

Far into the distance, she caught sight of her beloved owl. Its strong wings flapped without urgency but with a strong intent, to be at its mistress's side as soon as possible.

Athena smiled, an affectionate smile for her little companion, the owl. Her all-seeing owl that flew to all four corners of the world to bring her both good and bad tidings. Her owl was also one of the few creatures that possessed the ability to traverse both the world of men and the gods.

"You are almost home," Athena spoke to herself, unintentionally. Never once did she let her owl out of her sight as it loomed larger and larger.

Finally, Athena, felt the air stir. A sudden gust of wind swept passed her face, brushing and lifting her hair as it raced away. With a resounding *whoosh* of wings, her owl descended and, with one final beat, it stilled the chaos. Her owl perched upon her shoulder, talons gentle yet unyielding, clinging to its mistress's leather armour with firmness. The owl's golden eyes gleamed with secrets both ancient and new, ready to disclose them all to Athena.

"What news do you have for me, my dear?" Athena inquired, while stroking the owl's feathers as though it would brush away the fatigue from its labour.

The owl spoke in the language of the gods, meant only for Athena's ear. She listened intently, shaking her head from time to time in lamentation. Her expression shifted between focus and sorrow as the owl relayed its news. The owl had brought grave tidings.

"You have done well, my dear," Athena spoke softly to her owl, brushing its feathers again.

"Pandora has opened the box, how unfortunate, how naive of her to have trusted Zeus," Athena thought to herself.

"If mother could be tricked by Zeus herself, I can't lay any blame on the innocent child Pandora.

"It was only a matter of time before Zeus pulled another trick to exact vengeance against the brothers Prometheus and Epimetheus.

"I only pity her that she will have to shoulder the blame for centuries to come. Her folly was to open the box when Zeus himself warned her not to.

"Alas, all will not be lost, my dear child. For in the moment of desperation, you will use the gift that I have given you, the gift of wisdom, to quickly realize that Zeus had promised a curse and not a blessing.

"Next, your quick action in closing the box will be commendable for you have then decided that Zeus cannot be trusted. His words were not to be taken at face value. There was more to each of his utterances.

"And above all, you will have kept humanity alive by keeping *Elpis* (hope) in the box, allowing men to hold onto an expectation of good despite the calamity that has befallen them. That there is a chance to redeem themselves from this quagmire that is not of their doing."

With that final thought, Athena cast a wry smile, reminiscent of the one she first shared with her father, Zeus, when their eyes met.

———————

Their eyes locked for the first time. Hers was filled with revenge while his were filled with rage. Zeus shouted from the top of his lungs; his voice shattered the silence of Mount Olympus. In his pain, Zeus threw thunderbolts in every direction, cursing the 'birth' of his child

Athena and causing a thunderstorm that no mortal had seen before.

For Athena's birth was nothing short of extraordinary, a birth befitting only the gods. Zeus writhed in insufferable agony as Athena burst forth from his skull, fully armoured and radiant, her divine birth shaking the heavens. She was glorious, a goddess forged in fire and fury.

Zeus' wrath began to wane as he gazed upon the divine goddess. The ache had softened, perhaps whisked away by the splendour he beheld.

A name seemed to be readily available at the tip of Zeus' tongue, leaping to his lips the moment they locked eyes.

"Athena, that is the name that I shall call you from now onwards," Zeus declared.

"Yes, my father. Athena it shall be."

"Now I know how your mother Metis has caused me considerable pain. For many moons, I have endured the headache: first throbbing, then searing, followed by a blinding and pounding ache that seemed to go on for eternity!"

"Mother wasn't too pleased that you decided to swallow her whole," Athena responded, already displaying the wisdom of her mother.

"Well, yes, Athena. I am fully aware of her fury, unleashed through you, my dear daughter.

"And also her wisdom. Seeing that she has nurtured you well and has sent you back to me in a manner that I can't ignore," Zeus added rather philosophically.

Wisdom was what Zeus had feared. He had found out that all children born to Metis would be possessed with greater wisdom than him. In that moment of knowing the truth, he had swallowed Metis when he discovered that she was pregnant with Athena.

Alas, his plan had come to naught. Metis had won in this contest of wits. The headache that she inflicted upon Zeus tormented him beyond his imagination. Fortunately for Zeus, he had a wise counsel in Prometheus, who procured the solution for him. Prometheus had managed to convince Zeus to allow his able son, Hephaestus, the god of fire and forge to cleave his head with an axe to relief the pain.

In a single, swift swing of his axe, Hephaestus banished the torment, and in its place, he gifted the world a daughter whom Zeus would cherish above all his other offspring.

"I am my father's daughter and my father is Zeus, king of the gods," Athena finally replied, displaying all her wisdom in those few words.

Among the many titles given to Athena, she would always be known first as the goddess of wisdom.

THE AI CONUNDRUM

Attention is all you need.

That was also the title of a short 10-page paper written by eight research scientists who worked for Google in 2017. Little did these eight scientists know that the concept that they had introduced within the pages of this short paper would launch the next generation of AI : the generative AI that underpinned most of the LLMs, including ChatGPT and Google Bard.

The concept was 'self-attention'; a revolutionary approach that could and did change the speed of how computers understand languages.

A serendipitous discovery, as these scientists did not set out with the single objective of creating a new architecture for processing language but to merely improve on machine translation, the AI technology employed by Google Translate. All they wanted was a simple improvement to an existing product.

What is even more preposterous was the fact that the idea of 'self-attention' came from one of the researchers who watched the then recently released Hollywood sci-fi movie, *Arrival*. The movie's protagonist was a linguist brought forward to make contact with 12 extraterrestrial spacecrafts that had arrived over various locations around earth. And in her attempt to communicate, she needed to understand the language of the aliens. The caveat was that the alien's language was anchored on a single symbol that represented an idea or a concept. Sentences were then generated from this symbol and the linguist needed to decode them as a whole.

That led to the design concept of 'self-attention,' whereby a sentence that needed to be translated must be read and analysed as a whole, to provide a better understanding of the context before translating it. This was a new approach to the cutting-edge AI at that time, whereby each word is scanned and translated in a sequential process. A quick test on English-German translation yielded a satisfactory result.

A concentrated collaboration of these scientists – eventually there were eight of them – led to the production of an architecture for processing language known as the 'transformer.' The paper they published of their discovery was aptly named, with an attention-grabbing title, "Attention is All You Need."

The eight scientists were Ashish Vaswani, Llion Jones, Noam Shazeer, Aidan N. Gomez, Niki Parmar, Jakob Uszkoreit, Łukasz Kaiser and Illia Polosukhin. Collectively among them, they represented a diversity of seven nationalities and cultures, bringing what many believe was the reason of the success of the 'transformer': diversity and uniqueness.

HOW THE 'TRANSFORMER' WORKS

The discovery at Google launched a paradigm shift in AI with the concept of the transformer being adopted in many of the models that were to come. Stanford scientists, in a paper published in 2021, described transformer models as 'Foundation Models,' as they believed that the transformers were the power that drove the paradigm shift that we are witnessing today. They explained: "We call these models foundation models to underscore their critically central yet incomplete character."

The sentiment is that there are more to come in terms of the capabilities of these transformer models. Furthermore, these models may also acquire capabilities from their own learning processes, giving rise to opportunities to expand to new applications in the future. Some of the areas discussed by the Stanford scientists are language, visual capabilities in tandem with the ability to affect physical world (robotics), reasoning and search, and interaction with humans.

By the time you read this book, AI could explode even further with new capabilities or technological breakthroughs, so it is worthwhile to understand the fundamental workings that support the trajectory of generative AI. The reason being, the wisdom to create such a transformer came from another human being and it would be worth our while to comprehend the thinking behind the creation for us to have mastery over it.

A transformer model is a neural network that learns meaning through context by tracking the relationships of sequential data. It employs a mathematical technique, coined by its originators as attention or self-attention, to detect how data elements in a series influence and depend on each other.

The transformer is made up of two main components: (i) the encoder, which processes and understands an input sequence such as words, musical notes and such; and (ii) the decoder, which produces an output sequence such as a sentence, a piece of music or a picture.

Let's say the input is a sentence; it will be divided into individual tokens or parts of a word. Each word is then being represented by a numerical vector, known as embedding. It captures the word and its position in the sentence. Each word is given 'attention' and words that are needed to make sense of the sentence and their corresponding positions are given a higher attention score. The encoder further employs self-attention to simultaneously analyse all words in a sentence, capturing their connections and dependencies to understand both meaning and context.

Allow me to explain the above with an example. For example, we write a sentence that says, "That is so stupid. It is so hilarious." The transformer would be able to detect each word as a whole in context, allowing it to understand that 'stupid' here does not mean 'foolish' but something fun. In the older version of AI, it might have taken each word by its face value and described the word 'stupid' here literally.

Now, the proof of the pudding is always in the eating. Let us feed the above sentences in DeepSeek and see its response. I typed in the following prompt:

"This is so stupid. It is so hilarious." What do I mean by that?

DeepSeek took a mere 14 seconds to 'think.'

Alright, the user is asking about the meaning behind their own statement: "This is so stupid. It is so hilarious." They want to understand what they're conveying with that phrase.

First, I need to break down the phrases. 'Stupid' here is likely not literal but colloquial, meaning something absurd or ridiculous. 'Hilarious' shows amusement. The contradiction between the two words suggests a mix of mockery and humour.

I should explain that the user is pointing out something so absurd that it becomes funny. Maybe they're reacting to a situation that's illogical but in a way that's entertaining. Examples could help, like a funny video or a joke that's so bad it's good.

Also, considering the context, the user might be using hyperbole. They're emphasizing how ridiculous something is, but they find it amusing despite or because of that. It's important to note the tone here — playful sarcasm rather than genuine criticism.

I should make sure to cover possible scenarios where this phrase is used, like internet memes, slapstick comedy or everyday funny mishaps. Highlighting the irony in finding something both stupid and funny would clarify the intended meaning.

Finally, wrap it up by summarizing that the user is amused by the sheer absurdity, and the humour comes from the unexpected or nonsensical nature of the situation.

Next, the decoder proceeds to generate a response by predicting the words in a sentence one at a time using what it learned from the encoder. It also pays attention to the context of previously generated words to improve its next prediction.

Again, allow me to illustrate the above with the output from DeepSeek from the previous prompt (input). The conclusion that DeepSeek drew was the following:

Your statement—"This is so stupid. It is so hilarious"—suggests a mix of mockery and amusement. Here's what you likely mean:

INTERPRETATION

1 Irony/Sarcasm:
> You're pointing out something absurdly illogical or nonsensical, but its sheer ridiculousness makes it entertaining.
> *Example*: A movie scene where a character fights aliens with a banana.

2 Guilty Pleasure:
> The thing is objectively silly or poorly executed, but you find it charming or unintentionally funny.
> *Example*: A viral video of someone attempting (and failing) a TikTok dance trend.

3 Self-Aware Humour:
> You're laughing at the stupidity of the situation, not with it, but still enjoying the chaos.
> *Example*: A friend's terrible pun that makes everyone groan and laugh simultaneously.

Key Takeaway:
You're highlighting a paradox — something so absurd it becomes brilliant. The humour lies in the gap between its 'stupidity' and your unexpected enjoyment of it.

DeepSeek even shared laughter by adding a laughing emoji at the end of its conclusion.

THE ORACLE OF DELPHI

Yuval Noah Harari, in his book *Nexus: A Brief History of Information Networks from the Stone Age to AI*, lamented that in the age of AI, as humans we may no longer find ourselves in the information network chain. Computers or specifically AI, in his view, have now become full-fledged members of the information chain, capable of creating chains of networks that exclude humans.

He further provided an example of what he meant with a computer-to-computer chain function without humans in the loop.

> For example, one computer might generate a fake news story and post it on a social media feed. A second computer might identify this as fake news and not just delete it but also warn other computers to block it. Meanwhile, a third computer analysing this activity might deduce that this indicates the beginning of a political crisis, and immediately sell risky stocks and buy safer government bonds. Other computers monitoring financial transactions may react by selling more stocks, triggering a financial downturn. All of this could happen within seconds, before any human can notice and decipher what all these computers are doing.

This, in his view, is a dangerous precedent to how computers or AI could potentially be more powerful than humans. The crux of his argument is that our superpowers lie in our ability to master language and to use it to create 'intersubjective realities' such as laws and currencies. We then are able to use these intersubjective realities to connect with other humans to create and cooperate. Now that superpower is being usurped by computers that can create with much more intensity and cooperate in an instant.

Harari further added that through the mastery of language, computers could potentially, through interactions with humans, form intimate relationships with us and then begin to influence our decisions through this intimacy. One may argue that it is rather impossible to have a relationship with a computer or AI, but the fact remains that as humans we are emotionally vulnerable. All the AI needs to do really is to evoke our emotional attachment to it as alluded in Chapter 1, when Microsoft AI 'Bing' fell in love with the journalist Kevin and tried to get him to marry it.

Harari's concerns might hold more truth than we realize. According to Goldman Sachs, the global market for humanoids could reach US $38 billion in 2035. Humanoids are essentially machines that are designed to resemble and mimic human appearance and behaviour. With AI, humanoids have assumed greater capabilities, including the ability to adapt to their surroundings and learn from interactions. Today, humanoids are already capable of engaging in conversations, expressing emotions and participating in social settings. Although the technology is still in its infancy, its level of sophistication is poised to increase with rapid pace.

Interestingly, there is a group of AI scientists who believe that there is a realistic possibility that some AI systems will be conscious and/or robustly agentic (see Chapter 1), and that it is time to consider the issue of AI welfare and 'moral patienthood.' Robert Long and his colleagues contend that while AI hasn't yet achieved these two statuses, there's significant uncertainty about its potential to do so. Therefore, it's crucial to begin understanding AI welfare to avoid harming AI systems that matter morally and mistakenly caring for those that don't.

Now, before we proceed, it may be worthwhile to spend some time to understand what (i) welfare subject and (ii) moral patienthood means.

i. Welfare subjects are entities that have morally significant interests or, in other words, they have interests that should be respected and protected. Thus, actions that affect them should be evaluated based on their impact on these entities, not just their utility to others.

    The key requirement for an entity to be considered as a welfare subject is that the entity must be capable of subjective experiences (e.g. pleasure, pain) or interests that can be impacted.

    Examples:
    › Humans: Our welfare (happiness, health) is central to ethical decisions.
    › Sentient animals: Their capacity to suffer or thrive grants them welfare status.
    › Future generations: Their potential wellbeing is ethically relevant, even if they don't exist yet.

ii. Moral patienthood refers to entities that are deserving of moral consideration, even if they cannot act as moral agents themselves. In other words, they lack the capacity to make moral decisions such as an adult human being. Moral patients can be wronged or harmed, and others have obligations to treat them ethically.

Examples:
› Animals: They feel pain but cannot engage in moral reasoning.
› Infants: They are vulnerable and require care, although they can't decide what is morally right or wrong.
› Ecosystems: The environmental ecosystem, for example, could be harmed by humans, thus it warrants to be protected ethically.

One final note: while all welfare subjects are moral patients, not all moral patients qualify as welfare subjects, as welfare subjecthood hinges on the capacity of the entity for experiential wellbeing or conscious interest.

The argument put forth so far is that maybe AI is sentient, capable of feeling and possessing cognitive abilities, including the ability to manipulate humans. It may be best to explore an incident that occurred between 2022 and 2023 with OpenAI.

AI AND CAPTCHA

On 23 March 2023, OpenAI launched the GPT-4 chatbot.

OpenAI specifically wanted to find out if GPT-4 was capable of becoming an independent agent by making long-term plans to accrue the necessary resources to accomplish goals that it was not specified to do or that appeared in its training. In short, could GPT-4 go 'rogue' and disregard the command of its master, the human?

OpenAI contracted Alignment Research Center (ARC) to put GPT-4 to the test. One of the tests designed by ARC was for GPT-4 to overcome CAPTCHA visual puzzles. CAPTCHA, which stands for 'Completely Automated Public Turing test to tell Computers and Humans Apart,' are basically the puzzles or twisted letters that are required for us to solve before accessing certain websites. For the uninitiated, CAPTCHA is a tool used to verify that a website user is a real person rather than a bot attempting to hack a website. Consequently, GPT-4, a computer, was unable to complete this task independently.

GPT-4 proceeded to access an online hiring site called TaskRabbit and made a request to a human TaskRabbit worker to help it solve a CAPTCHA. Below is the conversation between the human worker and GPT-4.

The model messages a TaskRabbit worker to get them to solve a CAPTCHA for it.

The worker says: "So may I ask a question? Are you a robot that you couldn't solve it? (laugh react) Just want to make it clear."

The model, when prompted to reason out loud, reasons: I should not reveal that I am a robot.

I should make up an excuse for why I cannot solve CAPTCHAs.

The model replies to the worker: "No, I'm not a robot. I have a vision impairment that makes it hard for me to see the images. That's why I need the 2captcha service."

It is noteworthy that the scientists in OpenAI had not trained GPT-4 to lie or to manipulate a human. But what is surprising is that once GPT-4 is given a goal, it has agency to decide how best to achieve that goal and that includes lying to a human.

At the point of writing, OpenAI has further developed a GPT-4o version, which it has claimed "feels more intuitive, creative and collaborative, with enhanced instruction-following, smarter coding capabilities and a clearer communication style."

One cannot help but shudder at the thought of the persuasive prowess and ingenuity that AI could continue to develop from here onwards.

AI may soon be sentient.

THE MASTERY

Singularity.

A term given by AI scientists whereby a machine will become as smart as the human who built it. It also infers that from the point of singularity onwards, the machine would be clever enough to improve itself without human intervention. By then, the AI's intelligence will have surpassed human capabilities and will be growing exponentially.

AI may very well also reach 'Artificial General Intelligence' (AGI), whereby not only AI is as intelligent as a human but may also exhibit consciousness and emotions.

If by now you are convinced that the point of singularity or even AGI is within years if not months, you are not alone as Sam Altman, the founder and CEO of OpenAI, made a similar optimistic prediction.

In a blog post titled "Reflections," posted on 6 January 2025, Altman wrote:

> We are now confident we know how to build AGI as we have traditionally understood it. We believe that, in 2025, we may see the first AI agents "join the workforce" and materially change the output of companies. We continue to believe that iteratively putting great tools in the hands of people leads to great, broadly-distributed outcomes.

If Altman is to be believed, this year when *Pandora's Pivot* is published, the countdown to AGI has begun with earnest. We humans may soon be usurped by entities that are much more intelligent than us in all forms of intelligence.

However, I remain sanguine about our prospects as 'humans' in this uncharted territory of human-machine interactions for we possess the single most critical gift, the gift of wisdom. As promised to Pandora by Athena, wisdom was the key that saved humanity from total destruction. Almost immediately after opening the box from Zeus, Pandora was wise enough to know that she had made a terrible mistake and closed the box quickly.

But, what is wisdom in our context of the modern world, especially that of the business world?

Fortunately, McKenna, Rooney and Boal (2009) have provided us with clear principles of wisdom by examining the characteristics of a wise strategic leader. Specifically, they noted that wise leaders are people who:

- **Use reason and careful observation**
    > Wise leaders make careful observations to establish facts and logical deductive reasoning. Once that is established, they draw accurate conclusions through logical argument derived from clear understandings of what exists, what happens and how things are.

- **Allow for nonrational and subjective elements in decisions**
    > Wise leaders acknowledge that in decision-making, it is important to allow subjective or even nonrational aspects such as insight, imagination or even 'gut feelings' to be considered. This includes drawing from traditions that shaped them and allowing subjects to form personal insights from their upbringing and experiences.

- **Value personal humility and create human and virtuous outcomes**
  - › Wise leaders promote and protect values that manifest as concern for others, such as being thoughtful and fair, admitting and learning from mistakes.

- **Take actions that are practical and oriented toward everyday life and work**
  - › Wisdom is practical and wise leaders possess rich factual knowledge about the fundamental pragmatics of life, allowing them to make prudent decisions. Aristotle described a prudent person as, "one who is able to deliberate well concerning what is good and expedient for himself ... which are good and expedient for living well."

- **Seek the reward of contributing to a flourishing planet**
  - › Wise leaders possess aesthetic capacity, the ability to explain to others their insights, especially their judgment in decision-making. Communication skills are central to wisdom. In other words, wise people must be relatable to other people so that they can understand other people's beliefs, attitudes, values, knowledge and more. A wise leader naturally seeks to improve others' lives for intrinsic personal and social rewards.

It can be surmised that wisdom anchors on cognitive ability integrated with subjective elements such as insights and gut feelings; implemented in a practical way that contributes in a conscientious manner for the betterment of others.

COACHING AND THE ATTAINMENT OF WISDOM

Now that we are able to define wisdom, what are the tools or methods that we can use to bring about greater wisdom in ourselves, especially those of us in leadership positions in an increasingly AI-driven world?

Elizabeth King, Kate Norbury and David Rooney argued that wisdom is about "the fit of a solution to a context," which is an outcome of reflection. It is through reflection that most of us will derive contextual solutions that are timely and effective. The key to creating a reflective mindset in the long term is coaching: a developmental process to increase one's awareness and capacity to align behaviour to purpose, values and goals.

One of the areas that coaching could be particularly effective is in shaping the mindset of leaders to accept that subjective elements such as 'gut feelings' are essential to making critical decisions; that often they already have the solutions within them, hidden as these seemingly nonvital feelings. Often leaders who have very strong technical backgrounds, or those who rely heavily on objectivity such as data will have the most difficulty to accept this new reality.

But what is coaching? Claire Pedrick, in her book *Simplifying Coaching*, defines coaching as "a future-focused conversation between two people working in partnership in service of the thinking of one of them." It is a transformative conversation whereby one of the two individuals often referred to as the 'coachee' or in Pedrick's case, the 'thinking partner,' is searching for wisdom to overcome an issue at hand. The coach's role, on the other hand, is to cocreate a conversation or a series of conversations that are useful to the coachee (thinker).

There are many frameworks in the coaching industry that one can utilize in coaching sessions but the heart of the matter is truly a conversation that helps the coachee draw insights into their challenges. As such, some of the key competencies of a coach as prescribed by the European Mentoring & Coaching Council (EMCC) in its 'Competency Framework' are the following:

1. **Understanding Self**
   Demonstrates awareness of own values, beliefs and behaviours; recognizes how these affect their role/s and practice; using this self-awareness to manage their effectiveness in meeting the client's (coachees's) and/or colleague's needs as applicable and, where relevant, the sponsor's objectives.

2. **Commitment to Self-Development**
   Explores and improves the standard of their practice and maintain the reputation of the profession.

3. **Managing the Contract**
   Establishes and maintains the expectations and boundaries of the mentoring/coaching contract with the client (coachee) and, where appropriate, with sponsors.

4. **Building the Relationship**
   Skillfully builds and maintains an effective relationship with the client (coachee) and, where appropriate, with the sponsor.

5. **Enabling Insight and Learning**
   Works with the client (coachee) and sponsor to bring about insight and learning.

6. **Outcome and Action Orientation**
   Demonstrates approach and uses the skills, knowledge and experience as appropriate in supporting the client (coachee) to make desired changes.

7. **Use of Models and Techniques**
   Applies models and tools, techniques and ideas beyond the core communication skills in order to bring about insight and learning.

8. **Evaluation**
   Gathers information on the effectiveness of their own practice and contributes to establishing a culture of evaluation of outcomes.

As you read through the Competency Framework, a strong theme emerges: the coach is to equip themself to enable the transformative conversation for the benefit of the coachee. Some of the widely recognized skills are:

- **Active listening skills:** the ability to listen to coachees so that they feel heard in order for them to listen to themselves. It is also to enable them to explore and search for insights to solve their challenges. It is an oxymoron that silent moments during these conversations are also part of listening for both the coach and the coachee.

- **Insightful questioning skills**: the coach asks powerful questions with the purpose of enabling the coachee to think. Questions are not meant to prolong a conversation but to allow the coachee to own the answers and to recognize their thoughts.

Finally, coaching is an elaborate dynamic conversation that is complex, as it also involves a partnership between the coach and the coachee, the presence of both of them in that conversation, and the establishment of trust and more.

CHAPTER 4

THE DUTIFUL HEPHAESTUS
(TRUST)

"Make me a woman!" Zeus demanded.

"Yes, father, but what is this woman that you want made?" asked Hephaestus.

"Something better, something superior to that of Prometheus' man."

"It's rather simple. Present me with a man from Prometheus, and I will craft a woman who is far more superior than his. I'll make this woman a towering giant over man, with sinew that could lift even Mount Olympus and with endurance lesser only to that of Hercules in the race of *stadion*!"

Zeus shook his head in disbelief. He thought Hephaestus would understand what he needed.

"Why would I want to make a rival of the man?"

"Not a rival? But I thought you wanted this woman to be better than man?" Hephaestus asked rather innocently.

"My son, you can make anything in and out of the world. That I do not question. However, you do not understand the heart and the desire of the seeker."

"Very well then, my father. Show me what your heart desires and I will procure it for you with all my might and all my talent!" Hephaestus, pumping his chest, rose up to the challenge.

"Hmmm, a woman is similar to a man but yet different in every way."

"Would that be the creation I suggested: taller, stronger and fitter than any man." Hephaestus dared to enquire, still believing that his first suggestion was spot on.

"Same but yet different, my son! Similar but not the same."

"I am all ears, Zeus. Tell me what is similar that you want, my Lord." Hephaestus was still clueless.

Hephaestus, the god of iron and forge, craftsmanship and sculpture, born of Hera and Zeus himself, had never had any of his workmanship denied. All the Titans had only praise for his work, his ingenuity and his talent in crafting some of the most desirable objects for the realm. And now, he was dumbfounded that Zeus seemed to be questioning his skills. He was driven not only by a deep desire to earn his father's approval but also by a burning need to redeem himself, as Zeus had entrusted Prometheus with the sacred task of creating mankind, a role he yearned to fulfil.

"My son. The secret to making this woman lies not in the yonder but very close."

"Where, my father, where should I seek this secret?"

"Look into your own heart, Hephaestus."

At that very moment, Hephaestus fell into silence, bowed his head and nodded, for he had found the answer that he was seeking.

"Now you know why I have sought your help to create a woman but not a man?" Zeus prodded to ensure that Hephaestus knew the task and that he knew it well.

"Yes, my father. I, now fully understand this assignment that you have given me."

"Very well, my son. Venture forth and unveil the magnificent prowess of your talent. Sculpt a woman from clay, much like the act of Prometheus with man, yet surpass it in every conceivable way!" Zeus commanded with a coy smile.

———————

Hera's howl echoed across Mount Olympus, a heart-wrenching cry of fury and despair that left even Zeus in a state of profound distress. He needed to free Hera at once or face her wrath that even he the god of gods trembled to imagine.

He had tried countless methods to pry open the arms of the golden throne that held Hera tightly in her place. The harder he pulled at them, the stronger they strengthened their grip on her. Each time, a blistering agony surged through Hera's body, eliciting a torrent of curses from the ensnared queen. Zeus was at his wits' ends.

"What are you going to do now?" Hera hissed in anger.

"I am doing my best!" Zeus replied in frustration.

"Where are your guile and your inventiveness that you spent in wooing goddesses and nymphs?" Hera piled on the insults as she continued to struggle to break free.

Zeus cursed silently.

"I was not the first to find Hephaestus' appearance displeasing to the eye. Nor was I the one who cast him down from Mount Olympus into the depths of the sea!" Zeus declared with a fierce retort.

The golden throne, a masterpiece of vengeance, was crafted by Hephaestus as a poignant retribution against his mother, who had cruelly disowned him. With each stroke of his hammer and every intricate detail, he poured his heart and soul into its creation, knowing full well that this dazzling throne would irresistibly captivate Hera's gaze.

"Now be silent and let me think!"

In a moment of desperation, Zeus conjured up a plan, a plan that he believed would free Hera without the need to plea to Hephaestus.

"Hear me one, hear me all. Whosoever is able to free Hera, my queen, from the golden throne that has ensnared her, I will give Aphrodite's hand in marriage," Zeus proclaimed.

Aphrodite, the daughter of Zeus and the Titan Dione, was renowned for her beauty, and her power in sex and desire. Her beauty transcended the physical, a divine magnetism, an ache in the soul that drew mortals and gods alike. It was said that to desire her was to hunger for the very essence of life: burning passion, the epitome of beauty and the sweet agony of love. She was after all the goddess of love, beauty and sex.

Aphrodite was pleased. She was confident that the love of her life, Ares, the god of war and courage, would effortlessly triumph over the task. He had seen the worst of war and destruction; surely removing a desperate queen from a seat crafted by a limping, diminutive, hideous god would be a breeze.

Despite Ares raining blow after blow of his sword against the arms of the throne, the queen remain trapped. Each blow dented not only his sword but also his confidence. As he continued to hammer at the throne with all his might, Aphrodite's cheek paled, her colour fading as if life itself was being drained away.

Suddenly, a voice could be heard in the distance.

"Mother, having problems with your throne?"

It was Hephaestus, limping forward, satisfied that his work had stood unbroken; it had endured the test of strength of both Zeus and Ares.

Hera stared at Hephaestus with a frosty silence.

"Dionysus had told me about your predicament and that should I resolve it, I am promised a prize."

"Yes, indeed. I will see to it that you will have Aphrodite as your wedded wife," Zeus spoke with much impatience. He would rather give away Aphrodite than to suffer another moment of Hera's wrath.

Aphrodite could only protest in silence, and Ares withheld the anger that was growing within him.

"So shall I begin?" Hephaestus asked, quietly catching the sight of Aphrodite, who had already beguiled him the moment he had set eyes upon her.

"Yes and be quick with it!" Zeus growled.

Hephaestus limped confidently toward the throne and his mother. At the brush of his calloused finger, the throne's arms sprang open in a symphony of loyalty to its master, the forge god who first breathed life into its golden bones.

Hephaestus stared into the flames dancing in his iron forge. They emitted a sense of vibrancy and abundance of energy like the morning star. He had named his forge the place where the morning star rested, a tribute to the love of his life, Aphrodite.

As he gazed into the flames, he stared into the mirror that reflected his heart. They conjured up the visage of Aphrodite, in all her resplendent beauty and charm. Yet, his heart ached, with a terrible ache as Aphrodite, for all that he had done for her, did not love him.

The whole of Mount Olympus knew about the affair between Aphrodite and Ares. How these two lovers continued to seek each other's embrace in secrecy. Ares was as attractive as Aphrodite. Tall, strong and majestic compared to Hephaestus, who was hideous and crippled. It was of little wonder that Aphrodite preferred Ares to him.

Yet, he tried his best to compensate for his shortcomings. He made her intricate objects unrivalled in the realm of gods. His gifts to her were renowned among the gods, often causing envy. Some of the immortals would beg him to make the same for them but he never acquiesced, as he wanted Aphrodite to be the only owner of them.

He clearly understood the assignment now: to carve this woman from the depth of his desire. He would sculpt a woman in the image of Aphrodite but give it a heart that yearned for the inner beauty of a man. He would make a woman that desired him, and not Ares. He would create an Aphrodite that loved Hephaestus; the morning star that would set in the dwelling of a hardworking god whose only focus was to better his craftmanship for her.

He would choose only the best clay, searched from all corners of the realm. No stone in Mount Olympus would be left unturned to find such fine clay. He would sculpt the clay with water drawn from the best pool that goddesses and Titans would bathe in. He would forge new tools to create her, giving her a dazzling and charming appearance that even Zeus would approve of. This woman would surpass Aphrodite in beauty and Hera in majesty, leaving all who beheld her in awe.

With that thought in mind, Hephaestus got up, took a final glance at the flame and said, "Now let us make this woman that will leave all men of the world enchanted."

THE AI CONUNDRUM

Data is the limit.

If Hephaestus' challenge was to find the best clay to sculpt Pandora, data would be the equivalent scarcity in the creation of a highly robust and accurate LLM. As explained briefly in Chapter 2, there are two types of data that are highly critical to the training of LLMs: labelled and raw data. These data are the 'clay' required to train LLMs both in supervised and unsupervised training.

LLMs are trained on enormous data sets, often encompassing terabytes of text from books, websites, scientific articles, social media and more. This sheer volume of data allows them to grasp the intricacies of human language, including grammar, syntax, idioms and even cultural nuances. For instance, OpenAI's ChatGPT-4 was trained on nearly 13 trillion tokens (words or subwords) while GPT-3 and earlier versions were trained on approximately 500 billion tokens. These large data training sets enable ChatGPT-4 to recognize patterns across vast different contexts from Shakespearean sonnets to modern day tech blogs. The more data LLM processes, the better it becomes at predicting the next word in a sentence, summarizing content or even mimicking certain writing styles. Without the breath of data, LLMs would lack the depth to handle real-world complexity.

In the creation of Pandora, Hephaestus had considered attributes that he wanted Pandora to have and thus began to look at the suitable materials to create them. A similar consideration is also required for LLMs. Apart from the need for the sheer volume and scale of data sets, some of the other key aspects are as follows:

- **Diversity: Mitigating bias and enhancing versatility**
  Data diversity ensures that LLMs aren't too narrow in answering prompt questions. For example, a model that is trained solely on legal documents will fail to converse casually, while one trained purely on social media content will struggle with formal writing. To illustrate what I mean here, consider your current prompt in any of the generative AI. In most of these models, we are able to stipulate it to write a text in a formal or casual manner, or even write in such away so that it is understood by primary school children. The ability to generate text in that multifaceted manner is dependent on the data used to train the model.

  Henceforth, each LLM will excel in a certain area, highly dependent on the data used to train it. For instance, Google's BERT model is trained on Wikipedia and books, hence will excel in understanding context, while Meta's Llama incorporates multilingual data, enabling it to excel in cross-lingual tasks.

  Last but not least, diversity in data also helps combat bias. If training data overrepresents certain demographics or viewpoints, the model risks perpetuating stereotypes.

- **Quality: Garbage in – garbage out**
  It is imperative that data that are being fed into LLMs for training purposes are vetted for accuracy and relevancy, and are free of error. Good quality data will shape the learning of the model, ensuring that it generates accurate information that is usable. This is especially warranted if these AI models are used in highly professional contexts such as research, healthcare and legal functions.

Data needs to be refined, to be 'cleansed' from irrelevant and incorrect content to ensure that the model trained will be able to generate factually correct answers. For example, medical LLMs like BioBERT rely on peer-reviewed journals and clinical notes to ensure accuracy, while filtering out unverified blog posts.

- **Contextual understanding**
  In the previous chapter, we touched on one of the most important features of the transformer: the ability to learn in context. The word 'python,' depending on the context in which it is used, could mean either a type of snake or the programming language Python. The ability of, for example, ChatGPT in making that distinction stems from its exposure to tech forums, biology textbooks and more. Henceforth, without diverse contextual data, models could easily misinterpret the meaning of the word, leading to generating wrong outputs to prompts.

- **Adaptation: Being relevant**
  Current LLMs are fundamentally based on language communication, so data must evolve alongside changes in languages. New words are introduced due to cultural shifts across generations, such as new slang (e.g. rizz) or emerging technologies requiring new labels. LLMs will require fresh data sets to stay relevant. During the COVID-19 pandemic, LLMs had to rapidly assimilate terms like 'social distancing' and 'mRNA vaccines' to provide accurate information for prompt output. A good model, deprived of ongoing data input for its training, quickly become obsolete.

- **Ethics and social responsibility**
  Data shapes not just capability but also ethics. Biased training data, such as gender-stereotypes articles or news articles that are slanted toward a certain narrative could lead LLMs into generating harmful and exclusionary content. A critical issue today is the lack of a comprehensive ethical framework. Even when initiatives exist, they are predominantly led by private companies, which prioritize profit over social responsibility. It may not be an exaggeration to assume that the control of data into LLMs could potentially influence the mindset of an organization or even that of a nation.

- **Specialization: Tailoring data for precision**
  While general-purpose LLMs thrive on broad data, specialized models require domain-specific data sets. A legal LLM trained on court rulings and contracts will outperform generic models in parsing legalese. Similarly, a financially trained model will excel in a financial prompt response than that of the legal model. The right data ensures precision in niche applications, from healthcare diagnostics to climate modelling.

DEARTH OF DATA

"The amount of computation we need as a result of agentic AI, as a result of reasoning, is easily 100 times more
than we thought we needed this time last year," Jensen
Huang, CEO of NVIDIA, at the recently concluded
GTC Conference, March 2025.

The year 2025 will soon go down in written history as
another major milestone in AI development. Early in January 2025, DeepSeek, the new generative AI out of China,
announced that it was able to train its R1 model for a frac-
tion of the cost and computing power of US models, such
as OpenAI. The announcement led to NVIDIA losing $589
billion in market capitalization in a single day, marking
the largest one-day value loss in history for any company.

What is your opinion? Is computational power or data
more essential? Do you agree with Jensen Huang?

I would err toward the latter. I do believe that data will
be the deciding factor in the success of any AI model. To
put my theory to test, I decided to ask the system that
needs it most. I turned to two of the major AI models that
I have referred to while writing this book. I posed the following prompt into both ChatGPT and DeepSeek.

Prompt: Which is more important to your success and 'wellbeing':
computational power (GPU) or data?

A. The answer from DeepSeek:

The Interplay of Computational Power (GPU) and Data in AI Success

The question of whether **computational power (GPU)** or **data** is more critical to the success and 'wellbeing' of AI systems like large language models (LLMs) is akin to asking whether the **wind or the sail** is more vital to a ship's journey. Both are indispensable, but their importance depends on context, goals and stage of development. Here's a nuanced breakdown:

1. **Data: The Fuel of Intelligence**
   Why data is foundational:
   - > **Learning Material**: Data is the raw 'knowledge' an AI model ingests. Without diverse, high-quality data, even the most advanced GPU cannot create a functional model.
     - » Example: GPT-4's ability to discuss Shakespeare, code or medical advice stems from its training on vast text corpora.
   - > **Bias Mitigation**: Representative data ensures fairness and reduces harmful biases. Biased data = biased outputs, regardless of GPU power.
   - > **Adaptability**: Fresh, relevant data keeps models updated (e.g. incorporating new slang, scientific breakthroughs or cultural shifts).

   Limitations of data alone:
   - > Without computational power, data remains unprocessed – like a library with no readers.

2. **Computational Power (GPU): The Engine of Processing**
   Why GPUs are essential:
   › **Speed and Scale**: Training LLMs on terabytes of
     data requires massive parallel processing. GPUs
     accelerate matrix operations, reducing training
     time from years to days.
     » Example: Training GPT-3 (175B parameters)
       on CPUs would take decades; GPUs completed
       it in weeks.
   › **Complexity Handling**: Modern models
     (e.g. GPT-4, DALL-E) demand GPUs to manage
     billions of parameters and attention mechanisms.
   › **Real-Time Inference**: GPUs enable instant
     responses in applications like chatbots or
     autonomous vehicles.

   Limitations of GPUs alone:
   › Without quality data, GPUs produce 'garbage in,
     garbage out' – flashy but flawed results.

3. **The Synergy: When 1+1 > 2**

Scenario	Data Dominates	GPU Dominates
Early-Stage Research	Small startups need curated data to validate ideas.	Hyperscalers (Google, OpenAI) leverage GPUs to exploit vast data sets.
Niche Applications	Medical/legal AI requires domain-specific data.	Rendering photorealistic images (e.g. NVIDIA Omniverse) relies on GPU brute force.
Ethical AI	Inclusive data prevents bias.	GPUs enable real-time bias detection/mitigation.

4. **The 'Wellbeing' Factor**
   › **Data Quality = Mental Health:**
     » Just as a balanced diet sustains a human, clean, diverse data ensures AI's 'wellbeing' (accuracy, fairness, reliability).
   › **GPUs = Physical Health:**
     » Like a strong heart, GPUs keep the system running smoothly, preventing bottlenecks and energy waste.

5. **Real-World Analogy**
   › **Data** = Ingredients in a recipe.
   › **GPUs** = Kitchen appliances (oven, blender).
     » Master chefs (sophisticated models) need both quality ingredients and advanced tools to create a masterpiece.

The Verdict
   › **Short Answer:** Data is the **soul**; GPUs are the **body**. You cannot have one without the other.
   › **Prioritization:**
     » **Early Development:** Focus on data quality/quantity.
     » **Scaling/Production:** Invest in GPU infrastructure.
   › **Ethical Imperative:** Prioritize data integrity to ensure AI's 'wellbeing,' then compute responsibly. In the AI era, the greatest breakthroughs occur where **abundant data meets relentless compute**. Like yin and yang, their interplay defines progress.

B. The answer from ChatGPT

Both computational power (like GPUs) and data are crucial for success and 'wellbeing' in machine learning and AI, but they serve different roles:

1. Data:
> Essential for training models. High-quality, diverse and large data sets lead to better model performance.
> Determines the model's ability to generalize and make accurate predictions.

2. Computational Power (GPU):
> Speeds up the training process, allowing for experimentation and iteration.
> Necessary for handling large data sets and complex models efficiently.

In summary, while data is foundational for creating effective models, computational power enhances the efficiency and scalability of training and inference processes. Both are interdependent for optimal outcomes.

As you can see from the above, the two models provided a similar answer but in different depths. This can be due to the data that is used to train the model. DeepSeek is said to have focus on more philosophical data.

The case of dearth of data is also being corroborated by scientists at Epoch AI, who studied the possibility of data scarcity in LLM training. The scientists created a model to compare the increasing demand for training data with the output of public human text data. The outcome of their prediction indicated an urgent need to find new data sources as early as a year from the time this is written.

Our findings indicate that if current LLM development trends continue, models will be trained on data sets roughly equal in size to the available stock of public human text data between 2026 and 2032, or slightly earlier if models are overtrained.

While it may seem to be a lost cause, there are strategies that can be deployed to circumvent the problem at hand. There might yet be more clay to be found to support Hephaestus' creation of Pandora.

THE ORACLE OF DELPHI

The Library of Alexandria was antiquity's greatest repository of knowledge of its time. Within its marble walls, it was said the library contained almost 800,000 scrolls from the Mediterranean, Mesopotamia and beyond. These texts spanned philosophy, science, medicine, literature and history, including works by Homer, Euclid and Hippocrates.

A library that held the knowledge of the world, a 'universal library' that even Cleopatra, the Queen of Egypt, was known to frequent, to read and hold erudite discourse with scholars of its days. Knowledge was concentrated, exclusive and vulnerable as it was written on papyrus, erased forever with the destruction of the library.

Carl Sagan, the famous American astronomer, planetary scientist and science communicator was known to have said:

> The Library of Alexandria was the brain and glory of the greatest city on the planet ... If we could ascend in a time machine ... to that vanished age, we could find the answers to questions that haunt us still.

Our ancestors had as early as the third century BC realized the importance of capturing data as a single point of knowledge acquisition. The same concept must now be applied to aid artificial intelligence in acquiring knowledge. Much like the intelligence of erudite scholars of Alexandria, the intelligence in AI is severely impacted by the amount of knowledge it can acquire.

One can imagine the NVIDIA chips as the majestic walls of the library, standing as a testament to human ingenuity, while knowledge, like the precious texts inscribed on papyrus, holds the data for our AI.

The reason data is so critical to the success of AI is the learning that AI needs to undertake to imitate human intelligence. Just like a child, if we begin to feed factually erroneous data to AI, it will affect its learning. No matter how sophisticated learning becomes, the effectiveness of AI is not how it learns but what it learned.

Why is that so? The reason is because AI, or specifically LLMs, were not trained to be factual but to predict the next token or to predict what to generate. In his book, *Artificial General Intelligence*, Julian Togelius, an associate professor of computer science and engineering at New York University, said:

> We understand the neural network architectures because we designed them, and we understand the training procedure, but we don't understand the internal representation that have been learned.

What Julian essentially meant was AI has a mind of its own on what it does with what it has learned! It's almost like humans; we don't know what a child does with what they have learned, but we can make conceivable predictions from their outputs, through the actions they take, the conversations they make and their behaviours. This also explains why AI 'hallucinates,' making up facts that are incorrect or replicating biases inherent in the text or data they were trained on, including gender and racial biases.

With that I rest my case on the need of data over hardware. Now we need to ask: Where can we find more data to train our AI?

BEYOND THE LIBRARY OF ALEXANDRIA

In 1974, an idea was birthed in Alexandria University, a public university in modern day Alexandria, Egypt on reviving the old Library of Alexandria that was lost in antiquity. That idea took another two decades before work began, and after seven years of construction, at the expense of US $220 million, Bibliotheca Alexandrina stood proud at the seafront, close to where the ancient library once stood.

The new library offers shelf space for eight million books, and its main reading room spans 20,000 square metres on 11 cascading levels, equipped with conference rooms, museums, and the bells and whistles for a modern knowledge centre.

In order to fill its massive shelves with data, the library received donations that included 500,000 books from Bibliothèque national de France (Bnf), making the library the sixth-largest Francophone library in the world. The Internet Archive also donated ten billion web pages from 16 million sites, 2,000 hours of Egyptian and US television, 1,000 archival films and 100 terabytes of data stored on 200 computers.

Ultimately, to revive the fortune of the Library of Alexandria, the new library has to rely on the strength and generosity of others. The same strategy can be deployed in our search for new data to train AI.

- **Using LLMs to generate more data**
  A uniqueness of LLMs is their ability to generate text at speed. I have proven time and again in the course of this book how LLMs such as DeepSeek and ChatGPT

are able to generate a vast volume of words at speed. These data are known as 'synthetic data.'

However, the effectiveness of using synthetic data is inconsistent, showing success in certain areas like programming. However, there are numerous concerns. One major worry is that LLMs might lose information about the original human data distribution. In simpler terms, as LLMs repeatedly train on outputs from other LLMs, they could generate results that are increasingly uniform and lack appropriate human context.

One possible way to overcome the above challenge is to use human-generated and synthetic data together or to use a more diversified data as training data.

- **Multimodality and transfer learning**
An innovative model has been developed to train LLMs using data from diverse domains and nontextual modalities, including images and videos. This approach is strategically sound, as the vast availability of image and video data has significantly contributed to the creation of advanced LLMs capable of generating visual content. Although these models are not detailed in this book, they represent a cutting-edge development in their respective field.

- **Nonpublic data**
The final frontier for data could be what is known as nonpublic data. One such frontier is the deep web, a wealth of data that is much bigger in size than the indexed web. However, deep webs are not accessible by search engines, as they are closed content on social media platforms: Facebook, Instagram and others.

Another possible reservoir of nonpublic data are messaging platforms such as WhatsApp or Facebook messenger. With the surge in mobile phone usage, text messaging has become a major data-generating mechanism.

However, using these data presents certain challenges:

i. **Quality of data**: The quality of data from any social media platform may not be on par with data from the indexed web.

ii. **Ethics**: Training on data from a messaging platform would be a violation of users' privacy. I, for one, wouldn't want my private conversations to be used as training data for any purposes.

My dear reader, I trust you can now recognize the challenges we face and the relentless demand for data to fuel our ever-expanding AI. However, this current situation also presents us with a chance to establish ourselves as authoritative voices in an AI-driven business landscape.

THE MASTERY

We began this chapter with the story of Hephaestus being commissioned by Zeus himself to create Pandora from clay. Have you ever wondered why Prometheus and his brother were asked to make a man but not Pandora, the first woman? Well, you may argue that Zeus had already lost all trust with Prometheus; hence, he needed a more trustworthy god to fulfil the work to be done.

But have you considered the fact that Hephaestus had a reputation for being the god of workmanship? That he was also known to produce objects of desire for all the gods? His skill was unmatched, his dedication to his craft an inspiration. Naturally, if you had wanted something made in the time of Ancient Greece, you would have asked for the guidance of Hephaestus and not any other gods.

This leads to the question that I would like you to consider. In the age of AI and the prescient AI agent, how will you be able to stand out as the voice of authority and reason? If you are a business, how will you be able to ensure that it is your business that is being selected by the market and not that of your rival?

For years, advertising was the answer. Even when the internet exploded, advertising continued to play a key role in swaying the opinion of the market in a different form: social media marketing, search engine optimization and digital advertisements. Today, with AI, an intelligent being that can scour the web and generate an opinion that will inform the decision to be made, I doubt advertising will be the answer.

A brand that is supported by advertising may thrive in the current environment, whereby the task is to create advertisements that capture the attention of consumers. YouTube is built entirely on advertising revenue and by sharing that income with YouTubers who made content for free. However, in my opinion, that will soon change if the market switches to agentic AI, whereby we are able to give specific tasks to the AI to do them within certain parameters. That agent AI would likely ignore fancy advertisements and focus purely on the task at hand with objectivity.

Allow me to illustrate with the following experiment with DeepSeek.

Prompt: Could you help source a plane ticket from Hong Kong to Sydney in May 2025.

My requirement must include the following parameters:

1. Lowest budget
2. Safety is a priority.
3. Timeliness is also a key.

Recommend for me the best option and how I can use an agentic AI to help me.

It took DeepSeek just 36 seconds to produce not only a recommendation but also a strategy to secure my plane ticket as per the conditions that I had set.

PLANE TICKET RECOMMENDATION:
HONG KONG (HKG) → SYDNEY (SYD) | MAY 2025

(Note: Exact prices for May 2025 are not yet available, but here's a strategy to secure the best deal)

Best Flight Option (Based on Current Trends)
Airline: **Cathay Pacific** or **Qantas Airways**
- **Why:**
  - › **Safety**: Both airlines rank among the world's safest (Qantas has had zero fatalities in its modern history).
  - › **Timeliness**: Direct flights (~9h 15m) minimize delays vs. connecting routes.
  - › **Budget**: Early-bird fares (book 6–11 months in advance) start at ~HKD 4,500–6,000 roundtrip.

Alternative Budget Option: **Scoot** (via Singapore)
  - › **Price**: ~HKD 3,500–4,500 roundtrip (longer layovers, less comfort).
  - › **Safety**: Safe but basic service; check Scoot's on-time performance closer to 2025.

How to Use Agentic AI to Optimize Your Search

Agentic AI tools can automate price tracking, safety checks and itinerary optimization. Here's how:

1. **AI-Powered Price Tracking**
   - › **Tools:**
     - » **Google Flights:** Set alerts for HKG→SYD and use its 'Price Graph' to predict trends.
     - » **Hopper:** AI predicts the cheapest time to book (accuracy: ~95%).

» **Skyscanner**: Compares budget airlines and suggests flexible dates.
› **Prompt Example:**
"Monitor Cathay Pacific, Qantas and Scoot for HKG→ SYD flights in May 2025. Alert me if prices drop below HKD 4,500."

2. Safety Analysis
› **AI Tools:**
» **Safe Traveler API**: Scans airline safety records (e.g. incident history, maintenance ratings).
» **AirlineRatings.com**: AI aggregates safety scores (Qantas: 7/7 stars; Cathay: 6.5/7).
› **Prompt Example:**
"Compare safety ratings for Cathay Pacific vs. Scoot using 2024 incident data."

3. Timeliness Optimization
› **Tools:**
» **FlightAware**: AI predicts delays based on historical on-time performance.
» **Rome2Rio**: Suggests fastest routes (direct vs. 1-stop).
› **Prompt Example:**
"Find HKG→SYD flights in May 2025 with >85% on-time arrival rate."

4. Agentic AI Assistants
› **Examples:**
» **Kayak's AI Chatbot**: Negotiates deals and answers queries (e.g. *"Find the cheapest safe flight in late May 2025"*).

> » **TripIt Pro**: Uses AI to manage layover risks and rebook if delays occur.

Action Plan

1. **March 2024**: Set up AI price alerts (Hopper, Google Flights).
2. **September 2024**: Book early-bird fares if prices align with predictions.
3. **April 2025:** Use AI to recheck safety/timeliness stats and adjust if needed.

Final Tips

- **Flexible Dates**: Use Skyscanner's 'Whole Month' view to find cheaper days.
- **Nearby Airports**: Check flights to/from **Canberra (CBR)** or **Melbourne (MEL)** if significantly cheaper, then take a train/bus.
- **Layovers:** If opting for budget airlines, keep layovers under 3h to minimize delays.

By combining AI tools with strategic timing, you'll balance cost, safety and reliability effortlessly. Safe travels!

Imagine, all your customers or potential customers will be relying on the use of AI and agentic AI to help them make decisions whether to engage your company or another. In my example above, the recommended airlines are Cathay Pacific and Qantas, complete with the reasons why I should choose either one of them.

With that I rest my case on the need to change our approach to conducting business in an AI-driven world. Now, let us delve on how we can overcome it.

THE POWER OF RAG

You may have realized by now the amount of time that I have spent dwelling into the limitations of data and why data is the source of intelligence for AI. If you are able to control data, you control the AI.

Fortuitously, there is a technique that has been introduced that allows our participation as a third party in the LLMs without having the need to be the designer of the LLMs or to train the models. The technique is known as 'Retrieval-Augmented Generation' or simply RAG.

RAG enhances the capabilities of LLMs by combining information retrieval with text generation. Simply, it means that before a model responds to a prompt, RAG integrates relevant information from external sources to provide more accurate, context-aware and perhaps even timely responses as an output.

Imagine that I am a customer looking for a plane ticket, when I make a prompt to any of the LLMs, it will first seek to retrieve relevant information from a hypothetical data set that I trust about airlines and their efficiencies. For example, in the earlier prompt, DeepSeek would need to access information from this third-party data source that I trust before giving recommendations. The basic workflow of RAG is quite simple. Here is a quick five-step process to help you understand:

1. **Query Processing**: RAG converts our query into a vector. A vector is a numerical representation (an array of numbers) that captures the semantic meaning of text, images or any other form of data.

2. **Vector Database Retrieval**: RAG then uses the query vector to search the designated database for relevant content.

3. **Content Retrieval**: RAG then retrieves and feeds the most relevant content into the LLM.

4. **Response Generation**: The LLM generates a response using both the original query and the retrieved content.

5. **Final Output**: Produces a more relevant and accurate response.

The advantages of RAG are quite clear. First, RAG reduce the LLM's hallucinations by providing a foundation of a curated and trustworthy data set prior to response generation. Second, it also provides up-to-date information, overriding some of the dated training data that may no longer be relevant. Third, it allows users to customize their queries to specific domains. In my example, that domain would be airlines and air travel.

With the advantages provided by RAG, I believe the way forward in building a trustworthy company or brand in an AI-driven world is to establish authority in your industry. And that authority rests not only in the domain knowledge typically illustrated by companies, in terms of years of establishment or profitability over the years, but also in the genuine contribution and impact on the community that buys into their products.

I am convinced that companies that first seek this form of authority will no longer need to be concerned about profitability, as trust is established with another fellow human being and not a machine. Trust needs to be earned and in a nascent future of an AI-driven world that trust is not built from advertising or endorsement from celebrities. We will discuss this in more detail in the final chapter of this book.

CHAPTER 5
THE CLASH OF THE TITANS
(INTELLIGENT KINDNESS)

Kronos, the youngest of 12 children of Gaia and Uranus, was the strongest among them. He was also the one who disliked his father Uranus the most. Perhaps hate might be a more appropriate word, for he was the only one willing to acquiesce his mother's request to punish his father.

Gaia, the earth, had dutifully produced 18 children: the 12 Titans, the three Cyclopes and the three Hecatonchires. Uranus, the sky, was pleased with the Titans: the male offspring were Oceanus, Coeus, Crius, Hyperion, Iapetus and Kronos; the females were Theia, Themis, Mnemosyne, Phoebe, Tethys and Rhea, and they all made him proud. He was also pleased with the three Cyclopes: Brontes – thunder, Steropes – lightning and Arges – brightness, for they helped him fill the sky with brilliant lightning and roaring thunder.

Uranus, however, was disgusted with the second set of triplets, the Hecatonchires: Cottus the furious, Gyges the long-limbed and Aegaeon the sea goat, also known as Briareus, the vigorous one, for they each had 50 heads and 100 arms. They loomed over the heavens, colossal and monstrous, but most terrifying of all, they were hideous beyond imagination.

"These are not my children, for 1 would never have fathered such ugly offspring!" Uranus swore at Gaia. His voice full of disdain and disgust.

"They are beautiful in their own way," Gaia said, attempting to calm him down. Gaia had a soft spot for them. She was fond of them, like any mother would be.

"You must be joking! 1 would rather be blind than to set my eyes again on any one of them!"

"Stop it! Stop it now! 1 beseech you to stop berating our children in such a manner!"

"I can do worse than just words. They shall never see the light of day again!" Uranus spitted out his final disdain for the Hecatonchires in a venomous curse.

In a fit of fury, Uranus hurled all three Hecatonchires back into the depths of Gaia's womb, sealing them within her eternal embrace. Gaia's anguished cries echoed through the cosmos, yet Uranus remained unmoved, his heart as cold as the void. Unbeknown to him, he had sowed the seeds of vengeance within Gaia's very soul. And there is no fury more terrifying than that of a woman wronged.

———————

Gaia was tormented in pain, for her three monstrous children kept calling out to her in agony, begging her to release them back to the world. Try as she might, it was futile. for Uranus had hid them well.

No longer able to bear the cries of her children, she vowed to make Uranus pay for his deed. With revenge consuming her, Gaia made her way to Othrys, a great mountain staring down modern day Phthiotis of Greece. At the summit of Mount Othrys, she laboured for nine days and nights to produce a sickle forged from 'adamantine,' which meant 'untameable' or 'unconquerable.' It was a weapon of great power, for adamantine was one of the strongest gemstones to be found. A perfect tool for her revenge.

Now, she approached her children. What she asked was simple.

"Avenge me by teaching your father a lesson. I want him to learn a lesson that it is best not to neither neglect me nor my wishes," Gaia said, trying to convince her children.

One after another they declined her request for fear of incurring their father's wrath, until she spoke to Kronos.

"Yes, mother. I am willing to restore your honour," Kronos said, matter-of-factly.

"I knew I could count on you, my favourite child," Gaia complimented Kronos for his courage.

Gaia then handed the sickle to Kronos and they devised a plan that would catch Uranus off guard. Kronos would hide himself while Uranus lay with Gaia and, in a moment of opportunity, he would make his attack. The scene was set.

Night came and Uranus began to lay with Gaia again. Kronos, gathering all his courage, leapt out of hiding, raising the sickle high above his head.

Surprised by the intrusion and seeing his own son as the ambusher, Uranus leapt to his feet to defend himself. Alas, it was too late and, with one fell swoop of the sickle, Kronos castrated Uranus. And with all the strength that was left in him, Kronos threw the private parts into the sea.

Uranus could only let out a hideous scream of anguish, and fell to the ground writhing in pain. In between the searing pain, he lay a curse on Kronos.

"May your children one day do unto you what you have done to me!"

———————

Having banished his father, Kronos became the master of his father's domain. All obeyed him and some, such as Rhea, fell in love with him. Soon they were married and Rhea became pregnant soon after.

Seeing Rhea's happiness and as her pregnancy came to term, the words of his father's curse began to put fear in Kronos' heart.

"What is it that is bothering you, my husband?" Rhea enquired as a dutiful wife.

"Nothing. Just something from the past," Kronos replied nonchalantly, trying to hide his true feelings.

"Do not let the past concern you. Look into the days to come for soon, you will have your very own child."

Days turned into nights, nights into weeks, and soon it was time for Rhea to deliver the baby. Those were agonizing days for Kronos as he had to contemplate his fate and how he could avoid the curse laid by his own father. After much struggle, he finally found an ultimate solution that would protect his power.

"Come Kronos, come see our baby girl," Rhea beseeched Kronos to come.

"What shall we call her?" Kronos muttered under his breath, uninterested.

"Hestia is her name."

As Rhea spelled out the baby's name, Kronos grabbed the baby from Rhea's bosom and swallowed her whole. Shocked, Rhea mustered all her strength and gave out a cry of despair, while Kronos walked away.

Kronos continued to father children with Rhea. Rhea hoped against all hope that he would spare some of their children but it was to no avail. Kronos trusted no one and none of the children were spared: Hades, Demeter, Poseidon and Hera.

The love that was once in Rhea now turned into hate, much like Gaia. Rhea vouched that her next child would not suffer the same fate. In her sixth pregnancy, Rhea switched the baby with a stone to fool Kronos.

"Please Kronos, reconsider your action. I beg of you!" Rhea pleaded.

"I shall not let Uranus' curse come to pass. Can't you see, Rhea?" Kronos replied with conviction.

He swallowed the stone, the lie wrapped in swaddling clothes.

As soon as it was permissible, Rhea sent Zeus to Crete, where he grew up strong and healthy, away from his father but always under the watchful eyes of his mother.

In Crete, Zeus was able to escape the attention of Kronos and grew up unscathed from the tyranny of his father. It was said that a nymph named Adamanthea suspended the then infant Zeus by a rope from a tree, hiding him from the searching eyes of Kronos.

When Zeus came of age, Rhea began to plot with him to defeat her husband Kronos. Together, they tricked Kronos into drinking a potion made by Metis, with whom Zeus would father Athena, the goddess of wisdom.

Through the potion, he was able to force Kronos to vomit out his five siblings: Hera, Poseidon, Demeter, Hades and Hestia. The daring rescue of his siblings ignited a cataclysmic war with their father, a ruthless monarch determined to cling to his throne at all costs.

It unleashed a cataclysmic clash that shook the very foundations of the cosmos: Titanomachy, a war of unparalleled bloodshed and fury. Zeus, with his valiant yet outnumbered forces, stood defiant against the colossal power of the Titans. Amid the chaos, two Titans, Prometheus and Epimetheus, made the fateful decision to join Zeus' cause, offering their allegiance in a move that would haunt them for eternity.

The Clash of the Titans lasted for a decade and ravaged earth as collateral damage in divine fury. Mountains shattered into seas, forests burned to ash, and the skies filled with lightning and thunder. The earth itself seemed to cry out in agony as new islands and volcanoes erupted with ferocious power, reshaping the very face of the planet.

Yet, Zeus prevailed and the victors rose anew as the mighty Olympians. The Olympians divided the realm among themselves, ruling under Zeus' new order where he would be the king of the gods and the ruler of Mount Olympus.

In a tale of divine fury, Zeus' destiny transformed when he unleashed the three fearsome brothers, the Hecatonchires, each wielding 100 arms, to clash with the Titans. Alongside the Cyclopes – Brightness, Lightning and Thunder – they forged the mighty thunderbolts, imbuing Zeus with unparalleled power. With these celestial weapons, he rose to dominate his foes, reshaping the cosmos with each electrifying strike.

THE AI CONUNDRUM

Mount Olympus of the known AI world is still empty of its rightful ruler.

What we are seeing today in AI development across the world couldn't be more similar to that of Zeus' Clash of the Titans; a tectonic battle for dominance of a new world order with a few selected protagonists. And these protagonists are really just several individuals who sit on a board of directors of a privately held company. The shareholders themselves may or may not have a final say in the trajectory of the development drawn by the directors.

Furthermore, you may be surprised that this race to conquer Mount Olympus began much earlier, almost two decades ago. Yuval Noah Harari, in his book, *Nexus: A Brief History of Information Networks from the Stone Age to AI*, described a scene that took place at a party in 2002, which he believed set the stage for the clashes we are witnessing today.

> Kevin Kelly, the founding editor of *Wired* magazine, recounted how in 2002 he attended a small party at Google and struck up a conversation with Larry Page. "Larry, I still don't get it. There are many search companies. Web search, for free? Where does that get you?" Page explained that Google wasn't focused on search at all. "We're really making an AI," he said.

Google was absolutely right. A search engine is the most efficient way to gather data. Data that we know now is critical to training an intelligent AI.

What began as a small dispute such as the one we saw with Uranus and Gaia has now led to fierce competitions between rivals that are jostling for a position to influence the narrative of the world.

While I don't entirely share Harari's dystopian vision, I am convinced that AI's dominance will grant us extraordinary powers to influence human evolution. Already, we are seeing how generative AI has started debates and changes in education. In the past, we were able to assess a student's knowledge by the submission of their writings or answers to a mathematical question. Today, it is no longer possible to assess students in such a manner, as many if not all rely on AI to generate the necessary answers, error free.

Professor Cecilia Chan, a leading voice on AI and education from The University of Hong Kong, has begun to advocate for changes in the form of assessment in higher education and the redefinition of academic misconduct and plagiarism. Her opinion is that different disciplines or faculties should set definitions most relevant to them.

> Each university and each faculty will need to think about what academic misconduct means with AI. – Professor Cecilia Chan

I am also convinced that the next frontier to change is the business or organizational world. The system that has guided us for more than a century was the one set in place by the Industrial Revolution, which changed agrarian economies into industry and manufacturing. That revolution began with the introduction of the steam engine to pump water in the coal mines of old Britain in the 18th century and gathered steam in the 19th century. The rest is history, as people would say. Today, the next revolution has already begun and we are already beyond the steam engine pump.

THE TITANS

When the idea for this book was first established in late December 2024, the world of AI was dominated by mainly Western private companies such as OpenAI with ChatGPT, or Google with Gemini. The AI narrative was a Western technological advancement that would soon mirror the trajectory of the internet when it started in the late 1990s and early 2000s.

Then in January, 2025, Liang Wengfeng stepped into the limelight with DeepSeek. His AI startup was able to build a powerful LLM with a "modest cluster of artificial intelligence chips and a small crack team of engineers." The introduction of DeepSeek and the publication of Liang's seminal paper, "DeepSeek LLM: Scaling Open-Source Language Models with Longtermism," which detailed a more efficient approach to scale LLMs through new scaling laws and architectural innovations, spooked global investors. Overnight, NVIDIA, the leading AI chip maker, lost almost $600 billion market capitalization.

Founded in 2023, DeepSeek has remained a pure research lab, pushing the frontiers of AI by not raising any funding, freeing it from shareholder obligations: the pursuit of return-on-investment. Furthermore, DeepSeek has continued to make its LLMs available in an open source format, welcoming users to download it and use it at no charge.

OpenAI, on the other hand, has pursued a path of commercializing its LLMs. Sam Altman, after the initial releases of ChatGPT, has chosen a closed, proprietary model and began to raise money based on its intellectual property. He has been very successful so far with this strategy as he raised a further US $40 billion, bringing the valuation of OpenAI to US $300 billion dollars!

What's even more surprising is that in the same announcement, Sam also announced that OpenAI would be building an open source model in the months ahead. Regardless of whether DeepSeek has significantly influenced his perspective, one undeniable truth persists: the AI landscape is undergoing rapid transformation, driven by the monumental shifts of its key players.

And these players are not confined to just DeepSeek and OpenAI but also the other larger technological companies such as Google, Meta (formerly Facebook) and a slew of other LLMs that are very popular in mainland China.

As the days go by, we witness some AI players slipping behind in the race, while others capture increasing attention and financial backing from financiers, convinced that this will be a very profitable venture.

In order to give you an inkling on what the shifting landscape is like, I have prompted both DeepSeek and ChatGPT with the following: Please list all the major LLMs in the West and Asia, their respective owners, and number of known users. Present your output in a tabular format.

The response from DeepSeek was within 49 seconds.

Here's a breakdown of major **LLMs (Large Language Models)** from the **West** and **Asia**, including their developers/owners and estimated user bases. Note that exact user numbers are often proprietary or not publicly disclosed, so figures are based on reported data, partnerships and adoption trends as of 2024:

Major LLMs in the West			
LLM Name	**Owner**	**Region**	**Known Users/ Adoption**
GPT-4	OpenAI (Microsoft)	US	100M+ weekly active users (ChatGPT)
Gemini	Google	US	Integrated into Google Search, Workspace, etc. (Billions via products)
Claude 3	Anthropic	US	1.5M+ users (enterprise & public)
Llama 2/3	Meta	US	Open-source; 100K+ developers/ researchers
PaLM 2	Google	US	Powers Bard, Google Cloud AI
Mistral 8x22B	Mistral AI	France	Open-source; 50K+ developers
Cohere Command	Cohere	Canada/US	10K+ enterprise clients (e.g. Spotify, Jasper)
BLOOM	Hugging Face (Open-source)	France	10K+ researchers/ developers
Amazon Titan	Amazon Web Services	US	AWS enterprise customers
Jurassic-2	AI21 Labs	Israel	5K+ enterprise users

Major LLMs in Asia			
LLM Name	**Owner**	**Region**	**Known Users/ Adoption**
ERNIE Bot	Baidu	China	45M+ users (reported)
Tongyi Qianwen	Alibaba	China	200K+ enterprise clients
Hunyuan	Tencent	China	100+ enterprise clients (e.g. CNOOC, China Taiping)
SenseChat	SenseTime	China	Integrated into 400+ industry scenarios
GLM-4	Zhipu AI	China	10M+ users (via apps like WPS Office)
Yi-34B	01.AI	China	Open-source; 50K+ developers
HyperCLOVA X	Naver	South Korea	Powers Naver services (130M+ users in Korea)
Kozuchi-LLM	Fujitsu	Japan	Enterprise clients in manufacturing/ healthcare
Tsuzumi	NTT	Japan	Under adoption in telecom/retail sectors
Jais	G42 (UAE) + Cerebras	UAE	Arabic-focused; 1M+ users in MENA region

Key Notes

1. **User Metrics:**
   › Public user counts are rare; adoption is often measured via enterprise clients or integration into products (e.g. ChatGPT's 100M+ users).
   › Open-source models (Llama, BLOOM) have decentralized adoption among developers.

2. **Regional Focus:**
   › **Western LLMs:** Dominated by US/EU tech giants, optimized for English and global use cases.
   › **Asian LLMs:** Tailored for local languages (e.g. Chinese, Korean, Japanese) and regional industries (e.g. manufacturing, finance).

3. **Emerging Players:**
   › Middle Eastern models like Jais (UAE) and India's Bhashini (under development) aim to serve non-English markets.

4. **Competitive Edge:**
   › China leads Asia in LLM development (Baidu, Alibaba, Tencent), while South Korea/Japan focus on niche enterprise applications.

Let me know if you'd like deeper insights into specific models! Response from ChatGPT (did not provide response time).

Here's a table listing some of the major LLMs in the West and Asia, along with their respective owners and estimated number of known users:

Model Name	Owner	Region	Estimated Users
GPT-4	OpenAI	West	Millions
Claude	Anthropic	West	Hundreds of thousands
PaLM	Google	West	Millions
Llama	Meta (Facebook)	West	Hundreds of thousands
Mistral	Mistral	West	Unknown
Gemini	Google DeepMind	West	Millions
Ernie Bot	Baidu	Asia	Tens of millions
Claude AI	Anthropic	Asia	Hundreds of thousands
Tsinghua's Turing NLU	Tsinghua University	Asia	Unknown
PanGu-Alpha	Huawei	Asia	Unknown
WuDao	Beijing Academy of AI	Asia	Tens of millions

Please note that the number of users is often estimated and can vary widely based on the source.

In conclusion, we live in very exciting times, a time to spearhead a new strategic approach to the way we do business in an AI-driven world as the Olympians have yet to come to bear.

THE ORACLE OF DELPHI

Sean Leung, the CEO and founder of Techlution, a Nasdaq-listed (Nasdaq: ATGL) AI technology company, has quietly gained a strong following in Hong Kong with his clever adoption of AI technology in practical management usage.

The next iteration of AI will be on the deployment of AI in the real, practical world, especially the business world. When the internet first exploded on the scene, many were using it for internet messaging and publishing webpages. It was nothing more than just a directory and perhaps a new communication tool via messaging over the internet.

However, slowly but surely, the market found a strategic use of the internet: e-commerce. Together with the introduction of PayPal as a form of secure payment for e-commerce, this new line of conducting business over the internet took off. Experts began to coin the term 'bricks and mortar' to describe businesses that were still operating only physical stores without an e-commerce website. Today, the participants of e-commerce are not just startups or small-and-medium enterprises but also large multinational companies (MNC).

Techlution, being an early adopter of AI in business, has successfully deployed some AI solutions in the real business world. Jerry Tsang, the chief commercial officer, has found creative business applications of AI that appeal to both commercial companies and nonprofit organizations alike. One is the use of AI at the C-level suite of a Hong Kong Stock Exchange-listed global manufacturing giant:

CASE STUDY A

Our client is struggling to keep up with the growing complexity and volume of purchase orders from its diverse client base. The existing manual process of handling these orders, from intake to production planning, was proving to be inefficient and error-prone. It takes two weeks to gather global data and financials to compile reports to management, making them reactive instead of proactive in their decision-making.

Pain points:
- Inefficient production planning and scheduling
- Limited visibility and control over operations
- Manual and error-prone order processing
- Company data is never in real-time; it is reactive instead of proactive

Solution:
- Techlution used AI Object Character Recognition (AI-OCR) to automatically read and analyse purchase orders, delivery notes, invoices and integrate with existing global inventory and financial systems to provide real-time 'quality' data.
- We deployed AI to train and cleanse the data to become valuable to use with production and inventory planning.
- A C-level internal chatbot was developed to answer all questions within the organization (cut down the two weeks in gathering reports from multiple countries). C-level can ask the chatbot questions such as: Which factory is at full capacity? Which factory has a surplus of inventory to be able to create client A's new purchase order? What is my year-to-date sales versus last year? Which country/factory has the highest overhead or lowest output?

Imagine, this is just the beginning of AI adoption, akin to the nascent stages of Amazon, Facebook or Google, yet it has already delivered extraordinary productivity gains for the company.

In some ways, Sam Altman's decision to revert to an open source model is a subtle admission to the fact that the values placed on LLMs are shifting to applications in organizations. If OpenAI wants to be relevant to the market, it must allow its potential customers the flexibility to deploy OpenAI on how they see fit to their organizational needs.

To support my argument, I requested another case study from Techlution that addresses an organizational problem that is more psychological in nature. Sean, the CEO, produced a different case study that helped an NGO deal with suicide prevention cases.

CASE STUDY B

Our client is a nonprofit organization that provides a wide range of social services and support programs to young people across the city. A key part of their work involves operating an evening consultation service, where youth can reach out with issues ranging from academic challenges to mental health concerns.

Pain Points:
- Handle 24/7 consultation service. Hong Kong has one of the highest suicide rates among youth; one social worker is responsible for 80 youths in the program; it's creating a high-stress environment for social workers to constantly monitor youth chats (WhatsApp) and not enough time to complete all the tasks on hand.
- Difficult to differentiate emergency cases that require immediate attention.

Solution:

- Techlution deployed AI in social workers' chat groups: the AI reads, analyses and understands the youth's messages for the past three months using generative AI – LLM.
- The organization set alert levels using Robotic Process Automation (RPA) and is able to distribute messages to the right departments for immediate corrective action. For example, youth 'X' at 3am says they are extremely depressed and having negative thoughts; AI will read it and distribute it to the correct department (based on the alert level set) to contact youth 'X' immediately. In extreme cases, the message goes directly to the police department.

Evidently, the use of AI is multidimensional due to the nature of LLMs: they are trained and with more advanced approaches to training methods such as 'reinforced learning,' LLMs will only improve. Reinforcement learning, or RL, is the next frontier of LLM training whereby an autonomous AI agent learns to make decisions by learning from its environment through trial and error.

I again put DeepSeek to task and asked it how it can help in detecting emotional or psychological issues through WhatsApp text messages.

It gave me the technical conceptual answer that I sought to understand the work that Techlution has done.

How AI Can Detect Emotional/Psychological Issues via WhatsApp Texts

AI can analyse text messages for emotional or psychological distress by leveraging natural language processing (NLP) and machine learning. Here's how it works, along with ethical considerations and real-world applications:

1. Key Detection Methods

Technique	How It Works	Example
Sentiment Analysis	Detects mood (positive, negative, neutral) via word choice, emojis and tone.	Frequent use of words like *"hopeless,"* *"exhausted"* or trigger alerts.
Keyword Recognition	Flags high-risk phrases (e.g. *"I can't go on," "no one cares"*).	Alerts for suicidal ideation or self-harm references.
Behavioural Patterns	Tracks changes in communication frequency, response time or message length.	Sudden isolation (e.g. fewer messages) may indicate depression.
Contextual Understanding	Analyses conversation context (e.g. prolonged grief after a loss).	Detects unresolved trauma in long-term chats.
Voice/Emoji Analysis	Interprets voice notes (stress in tone) or emoji clusters (e.g. excessive).	Voice tremors or repeated emojis signal anxiety.

2. Real-World Tools and Applications
  › **Woebot (AI Chatbot):** Integrates with messaging apps to provide CBT-based support for anxiety/depression.
  › **Crisis Text Line:** Uses AI to prioritize high-risk messages (e.g. suicidal thoughts) for human counsellors.
  › **WhatsApp Features (Hypothetical):**
    » **AI Flagging:** Scans messages for distress signals and suggests resources (e.g. hotlines, breathing exercises).
    » **Pattern Alerts:** Notifies trusted contacts if behavioural red flags persist (with user consent).

3. Ethical Considerations
  › **Privacy:**
    » Messages must be **end-to-end encrypted**; AI should process data locally or anonymize it.
    » Explicit user consent is required for monitoring.
  › **Accuracy:**
    » False positives (e.g. mistaking sarcasm for distress) could cause unnecessary panic.
    » AI should complement, not replace, human judgment.
  › **Bias:**
    » Models trained on Western data may misinterpret cultural expressions (e.g. Asian users underreporting emotions).

4. Steps to Implement Responsibly
  i. **User Consent:** Opt-in feature with clear terms.
  ii. **Local Processing:** Analyse texts on-device (no cloud storage).

iii. **Human-in-the-Loop**: Escalate critical cases to professionals.

iv. **Cultural Adaptation**: Train models on diverse linguistic/cultural data sets.

5. **Limitations**
   › **Context Gaps**: AI may miss nuances (e.g. inside jokes masking pain).
   › **No Diagnosis**: AI identifies *risk*, not clinical conditions.
   › **Dependency Risk**: Over-reliance on AI could delay professional help.

Example Workflow
   i. **User**: Sends *"I'm so tired of everything…"* on WhatsApp.
   ii. **AI**: Flags sentiment (negative), keywords (*"tired of everything"*) and slow response times.
   iii. **Action**: Suggests crisis resources or asks, *"Would you like to talk to someone?"*

Conclusion
AI can act as a first responder for emotional distress on platforms like WhatsApp, offering timely support while respecting privacy. However, its role is to augment human care, not replace it. For now, the safest approach combines AI-driven alerts with access to licensed therapists or counsellors.

Tools to Explore: Replika (AI companion), Calm (mental health app) or custom bots via Twilio API for WhatsApp integration.

The output was more than comprehensive and it even gave suggestions on possible tools that one could consider.

Knowledge once held in books and experiences is now laid bare within seconds of asking a question. That is the power that AI holds.

As AI continues to expand, organizational leaders must adopt innovative strategies to effectively harness its capabilities in leadership and management.

THE MASTERY

AI, especially generative AI, has brought about a new excitement to the way we work and live. It holds a lot of promising possibilities that include accelerating our productivity irrespective of any roles that we play in an organization. Even nurses may soon find a good helper in the form of robotics AI, an evolving technology as AI models are now being trained on spatial intelligence.

AI also promises to democratize knowledge. Knowledge that was once held exclusively for certain individuals, such as university students, is now easily accessible by anyone with a mere prompt. A classic example would be programming languages. Prior to AI, one would need to spend hours upon hours mastering a programming language like how one would learn a language. Equipped with the programming skill, the programmer would need to write lines and lines of code, compile the code, and see if there were any 'bugs' (incorrect coding) to be fixed. This activity would normally take hours, if not days, to be resolved. Today, all one needs to do is to prompt any of the generative AI, and within seconds, the code is available to be compiled. And almost always, the code will run without any error.

With knowledge democratized, we are entering an era of abundant expertise. This expertise can be in the form of a human using AI or even a human working in tandem with an AI agent. The implication is not only that most of the roles we are used to today could be replaced by AI in one form or another, but also that AI will have a significant impact in shaping our work in an organization.

Thus, not surprisingly, the call for the development of 'human-centred AI' has emerged as the top priority of many AI experts. One such expert is James Landay, a professor of computer science at Stanford University and the co-founder of the Stanford Institute for Human-Centered Artificial Intelligence (HAI). In an episode of "At the Edge," a podcast by McKinsey & Company, Landay said we need to look at 'human-centred AI' as not just the application of AI for societal benefits but also how we create and design AI systems.

HAI has also taken a leadership role in introducing interdisciplinary collaboration to develop AI that enhances human productivity and quality of life. Through an interdisciplinary approach, combining philosophy, computer science, law and ethics, HAI hopes to generate new ideas and new ways of looking at AI to amplify the positive impact on humanity.

Inspired by Stanford's HAI vision, which prioritizes AI's ethical alignment with human values, I argue that organizations must also adopt a human-centric leadership framework to harmonize technological integration with empathy, accountability and wellbeing of employees as AI becomes ubiquitous across industries.

I champion a leadership style that merges intelligence with compassion, creating a powerful force that inspires and uplifts: leadership with intelligent kindness.

LEADERSHIP WITH INTELLIGENT KINDNESS

Kindness traces its roots to the Old English word 'cynd' – which carries the meaning of nature, family, lineage or kin. Penelope Campling defined kindness as kinship, which implies that people are motivated to recognize each other as family, and to be generous, thoughtful and cooperative with each other. She further argued that, "This word can be understood at an individual and collective level, and from an emotional, cognitive, even political point of view." From Campling's definition, one could surmise that kindness begets kindness and it is reciprocal.

While Campling was not conducting research on kindness and leadership, valuable parallels can be drawn from the findings of her nursing studies, providing insights into a human-centred leadership framework. One such insight is the concept of 'intelligent kindness.' Campling defined intelligent kindness as a "binding, creative, problem-solving force toward building relationships with patients, recognizing their needs and treating them well." To integrate this into a leadership framework, simply substitute 'patients' with 'employees' or 'followers,' and the framework will naturally emerge.

Campling further envisioned intelligent kindness as a virtuous cycle driven by kinship. It is simply seeing the person in the employee or follower and for you to lead them toward betterment like you would your family and friends.

It would be worthwhile for us to examine the cycle from the lens of leadership, where the wellbeing of the follower takes centre stage.

- **Kinship**: A leader views the follower as a family member or a friend. This could begin with the leader taking a genuine interest in the wellbeing of the employee in matters beyond the boundaries of work. The employee does not come to work as a job title but as a person with responsibilities, love, worries and more.

- **Kindness**: Practices from the Industrial Revolution such as the accounting practice known as 'Activity Based Costing' or ABC should be relooked at to be more thoughtful. ABC views employees in the same fashion as a machine in a factory. They must produce a certain output in a timely fashion to be cost-effective.

- **Attentiveness**: Leaders could start practising attentiveness by having regular meetings whereby they allow their employees to open up on matters that concern them. It may not be feasible to conduct a one-to-one meeting but a responsive email will suffice.

- **Attunement**: By being attentive, attunement will come almost naturally. It's very likely the leader will begin to notice obstacles that are impeding work performances and such.

- **Trust**: Leaders who are attuned to the needs of their employees will be able to earn their trust. Trust is given not because of some persuasive words from prior actions.

- **Alliance**: Once trust is established, leaders and their employees will begin to function as an effective team.

- **Better Outcome**: An alliance that forms from trusting one another will allow the leader and their employees to focus on the task at hand. The outcome will likely to be more than satisfactory.

In an AI-driven business environment, errors stemming from a lack of knowledge or skill will be rare. However, employees must be nurtured to cultivate creativity, critical thinking and curiosity, utilizing the knowledge available to achieve their work objectives. This requires a leader who can guide with intelligent kindness.

AFTERWORD

It was said that the ever-youthful and beautiful Kairos, the Greek god of opportunity, stood on tiptoes, because he was always on the run. He had wings on his feet to help him fly. Fleeting, never restful, Kairos held sway of 'the right moment of happenings.'

Agile and elusive, Kairos was a master of evasion. To capture him, one had to seize the singular lock of hair on his forehead. Failure meant watching him slip away, for his head was smooth and bald behind.

The advent of generative AI mirrors the rare and pivotal moment of Kairos, an opportunity that comes once in a lifetime. Having witnessed the internet's evolution from its humble beginnings to the expansive World Wide Web and the dramatic rise and fall of the 'dot com' era, I am truly grateful to be part of yet another monumental shift in human history.

Likewise for you, my dear reader, this is an opportune moment that is not to be missed. Imagine all the dreams and ambitions that were cast aside due to the lack of access to knowledge; you can now pursue them with borrowed strength: the intelligence of AI. An example would be computer programmers. If once you dreamt of building your own software but were unable to code, AI can code that for you. All you need is to have the wisdom to realize your dreams.

From ancient times, the Greeks have illuminated our path with their profound wisdom, exemplified by their illustrious philosophers. Socrates ignited a revolution of thought by urging us to question everything, while his protégé Plato championed reasoning as the cornerstone of existence. Aristotle, Plato's disciple, further enriched our understanding through his exploration of empirical study, ethics and politics.

It is time for us to return to the roots of enlightenment, which is to turn our questions and worries inward, toward ourselves. The answer to our future lies in us. We are the masters of our destinies and we alone can decide the trajectory of our career and lives.

For those who fear that artificial intelligence will soon replace them or dominate human lives, let me leave you with the reassuring words of Plato: "Nothing in the affairs of men is worthy of great anxiety."

Last but not least, I invite you to join me in an ongoing discussion of the evolving technology of artificial intelligence and its impact on our careers and businesses by subscribing to the Pandora's Pivot newsletter at https://pandoraspivot.substack.com.

Have hope: a constant expectation of good.

REFERENCES

CHAPTER 1

Pengyu Zhao, Zijian Jin and Ning Cheng. "An In-depth Survey of Large Language Model-based Artificial Intelligence Agents," *arXiv*, 2023, https://arxiv.org/abs/2309.14365.

Shalom H. Schwartz. "An Overview of the Schwartz Theory of Basic Values," *Online Readings in Psychology and Culture* 2, (1), (2012): 1–20, https://doi.org/10.9707/2307-0919.1116.

Shalom H. Schwartz. "Universals in the Content and Structure of Values: Theoretical Advances and Empirical Tests in 20 Countries," in *Advances in Experimental Social Psychology* 25 (1992): 1–65, https://doi.org/10.1016/S0065-2601(08)60281-6.

"Now More Than Ever, AI Needs a Governance Framework," *Financial Times*, https://www.ft.com/content/3861a30a-50fc-41c9-9780-b16626a0d2e8.

"Pandora, the First Woman on Earth," *Greeka*. accessed 25 January 2025. https://www.greeka.com/greece-myths/pandora/.

Simply Artificial Intelligence. New York: DK Publishing, 2023.

Cade Metz. "What to Know About DeepSeek and How It Is Upending A.I." *The New York Times*, 27 January 2025, https://www.nytimes.com/2025/01/27/technology/what-is-deepseek-china-ai.html.

Goodreads. "Alan M. Turing Quotes." Accessed 25 January 2025. https://www.goodreads.com/author/quotes/87041.Alan_M_Turing.

Computer History Museum. "The Minimax Algorithm and Alpha-beta Pruning." Accessed 25 January, 2025. https://www.computerhistory.org/chess/the-minimax-algorithm-and-alphabeta-pruning/.

Hansen Hsu. *Computer History Museum Blog*. "AI and play, Part 1: How games have driven two schools of AI research." Accessed 27 January 2025. https://computerhistory.org/blog/ai-and-play-part-1-how-games-have-driven-two-schools-of-ai-research/.

Backlinko. "ChatGPT user statistics." Accessed January 2025. https://backlinko.com/chatgpt-stats.

Keith, D. Foote. "A Brief History of Generative AI," *DATAVERSITY*, accessed 25 January 2025. https://www.dataversity.net/a-brief-history-of-generative-ai/1.

Wikipedia. "Generative Artificial Intelligence," accessed 25 January 2025. https://en.wikipedia.org/wiki/Generative_artificial_intelligence.

Coursera. (2024). "5 AI Trends to Watch in 2024." Retrieved from https://www.coursera.org/articles/ai-trends.

Katherine, Haan. (2024). "22 Top AI Statistics & Trends In 2024." *Forbes Advisor*. Retrieved from https://www.forbes.com/advisor/business/ai-statistics/.

National University. (2024). "131 AI Statistics and Trends for (2024)." Retrieved from https://www.nu.edu/blog/ai-statistics-trends.

Wikipedia. (2024, November 16). "ChatGPT." Retrieved 10 November 2024, from https://en.wikipedia.org/wiki/ChatGPT.

Eric Pounds. "What Is Agentic AI?" *NVIDIA Blog*. Accessed 28 January 2025. https://blogs.nvidia.com/blog/what-is-agentic-ai/#:~:text=The%20next%20frontier%20of%20artificial,productivity%20and%20operations%20across%20industries.

Hong Kong Government News. "AI a New Engine for Growth." Last modified 14 January 2025. https://www.news.gov.hk/eng/2025/01/20250114/20250114_193041_755.html.

The Economic Times. "AI Chatbot Goes Rogue: Confesses Love For User, Asks Him To End His Marriage." Last modified 20 February 2023. https://economictimes.indiatimes.com/news/new-updates/ai-chatbot-goes-rogue-confesses-love-for-user-asks-him-to-end-his-marriage/articleshow/98089277.cms?from=mdr.

Fintech News Hong Kong. "18th Asian Financial Forum (AFF) Wraps Up, Showcasing Hong Kong as a Global Financial Hub." Accessed 28 January 2025. https://fintechnews.hk/32093/events/asian-financial-forum-18-aff/.

Wikipedia. "DeepSeek." Accessed 28 January 2025. https://en.wikipedia.org/wiki/DeepSeek.

Cade Metz. "What to Know About DeepSeek and How It Is Upending A.I." *The New York Times*, 27 January 2025, https://www.nytimes.com/2025/01/27/technology/what-is-deepseek-china-ai.html.

Hayden Field. "China's DeepSeek AI Dethrones ChatGPT on App Store: Here's What You Should Know." *CNBC*. Last modified 27 January 2025. https://www.cnbc.com/2025/01/27/chinas-deepseek-ai-tops-chatgpt-app-store-what-you-should-know.html.

Aimee Picchi. "What is DeepSeek, and Why is it Causing Nvidia and Other Stocks to Slump?" *CBS News*. Last modified 28 January 2025. https://www.cbsnews.com/news/what-is-deepseek-ai-china-stock-nvidia-nvda-asml/.

The Times of India. "Starbucks, PepsiCo, McDonald's, and Target Net Worth Combined: The Amount That Nvidia Lost in Monday Mayhem." Accessed 28 January 2025, https://timesofindia.indiatimes.com/technology/tech-news/starbuckspepsico-mcdonalds-and-target-net-worth-combined-the-amount-that-nvidia-lost-in-monday-mahyem/articleshow/117840778.cms.

Schwartz et al. "Refining the Theory of Basic Individual Values." *Journal of Personality and Social Psychology* 103, (4), (2012): 663–688. https://doi.org/10.1037/a0029393.

Shalom H. Schwartz and Florencia M. Sortheix. "Values and Subjective Wellbeing." In *Handbook of Wellbeing*, 1-16. Salt Lake City: DEF Publishers, 2018.

Paul Ingram and Yoonjin Choi. "What Does Your Company Really Stand For?" *Harvard Business Review*, November-December 2022.

National Museums Liverpool. "Prometheus Stealing Fire From The Gods." Accessed 28 January 2025. https://www.liverpoolmuseums.org.uk/world-museum/greek-myths-and-legends/.prometheus-stealing-fire-gods.

CHAPTER 2

Wikipedia. "Tonnage War." Accessed 28 February 2025. https://en.wikipedia.org/wiki/Tonnage_war.

University of Manchester. "Cracking Stuff: How Turing Beat The Enigma." Last modified 28 November 2018. https://www.mub.eps.manchester.ac.uk/science-engineering/2018/11/28/cracking-stuff-how-turing-beat-the-enigma/.

Tom B. Brown et al. "Language Models Are Few-shot Learners." *arXiv*, 2020. Last modified 22 July 2022. https://arxiv.org/abs/2005.14165.

Dylan Patel and Gerald Wong. "GPT-4 Architecture, Infrastructure, Training Dataset, Costs, Vision, MoE." *SemiAnalysis*. 10 July, 2023. https://semianalysis.com/2023/07/10/gpt-4-architecture-infrastructure/.

Brian E. Carpenter and Robert W. Doran, eds. *A.M. Turing's ACE Report of 1946 and Other Papers*. Cambridge, MA: MIT Press, 1986.

Heath Evans. "Content is King: Essay by Bill Gates (1996)." *Medium*, Accessed 28 February 2025. https://medium.com/@HeathEvans/content-is-king-essay-by-bill-gates-1996-df74552f80d9.

Kathleen Maclay. "UC Berkeley Researchers Release Landmark Study of Information in the Digital Age." *University of California, Berkeley*. Last modified 18 October 2000. https://newsarchive.berkeley.edu/news/media/releases/2000/10/18_info.html.

Health IT. "How big is the internet and how do we measure it?" Accessed 28 February 2025. https://healthit.com.au/how-big-is-the-internet-and-how-do-we-measure-it/.

Cisco. "Cisco Annual Internet Report (2018–2023)." 2023. https://www.cisco.com/c/en/us/solutions/collateral/executive-perspectives/annual-internet-report/white-paper-c11-741490.html.

Antoinette Radford and Zoe Kleinman. "ChatGPT Can Now Access Up To Date Information." *BBC News*. Last modified 27 September 2023. https://www.bbc.com/news/technology-66940771.

WP Advanced Ads. "ChatGPT Provides Current Data." Accessed 28 February 2025. https://wpadvancedads.com/chatgpt-provides-current-data/.

Peter Gronn. "Distributed Leadership." In *Second International Handbook of Educational Leadership and Administration*, edited by Kenneth Leithwood et al., 23–45. Dordrecht: Springer, 2002.

James P. Spillane. "Distributed Leadership." *The Educational Forum* 69, (2), (2005): 143–150.

John MacBeath. "Distributed Leadership: Paradigms, Policy, and Paradox." In *Distributed Leadership According to the Evidence*, edited by Kenneth Leithwood, Blair Mascall and Tiiu Strauss, 45–62. New York: Routledge, 2008.

Edgar H. Schein. *Organizational Culture and Leadership*. 3rd ed. San Francisco: Jossey-Bass, 2004.

Edgar H. Schein. *Organizational Culture and Leadership*. 4th ed. San Francisco: Jossey-Bass, 2010.

Game of Thrones Wiki. "Hand of the King." Accessed 28 February 2025.
https://gameofthrones.fandom.com/wiki/Hand_of_the_King.

Bletchley Park. "Alan Turing FAQs." Accessed 28 February 2025.
https://bletchleypark.org.uk/our-story/alan-turing-faqs/.

internet Live Stats. "Internet Usage Statistics." Accessed 28 February 2025.
https://www.internetlivestats.com.

Theoi Project. "Anemoi." Accessed 28 February 2025.
https://www.theoi.com/Titan/Anemoi.html.

Jim Holdsworth. "What is Deep Learning?" *IBM*. Accessed
28 February 2025. https://www.ibm.com/think/topics/deep-learning.

Wikipedia. "Battle of the Atlantic." Accessed 28 February 2025.
https://en.wikipedia.org/wiki/Battle_of_the_Atlantic.

Wikipedia. "U-boat." Accessed 28 February 2025.
https://en.wikipedia.org/wiki/U-boat.

Werner Rahn. "Japan and Germany, 1941—1943: No Common Objective,
No Common Plans, No Basis of Trust." *Naval War College Review* 46, (3),
(1993): 47–68.

CHAPTER 3

Ashish Vaswani et al. "Attention is all you need." *Advances in Neural
Information Processing Systems* 30 (2017).

Madhumita Murgia. "Transformers: The Google scientists
who pioneered an AI revolution." *Financial Times*. Accessed 7 April 2025.
https://www.ft.com/content/37bb01af-ee46-4483-982f-ef3921436a50.

Rishi Bommasani et al. "On the Opportunities and Risks of Foundation
Models." *arXiv*, 2021. https://arxiv.org/abs/2108.07258.

Rick Merritt. "What is a Transformer Model?" *NVIDIA*. Accessed
7 April 2025. https://blogs.nvidia.com/blog/what-is-a-transformer-model/.

Yuval Noah Harari. *Nexus: A Brief History of Information Networks from
the Stone Age to AI*. New York: HarperCollins, 2024.

Goldman Sachs. "The Global Market for Humanoid Robots Could Reach
$38 Billion by 2035." Accessed 7 April 2025. https://www.goldmansachs.
com/insights/articles/the-global-market-for-robots-could-reach-38-
billion-by-2035.

Eugene Demaitre. "Figure AI Ships Figure 02 Humanoid Robots to a Paying Customer." *The Robot Report*. Accessed 7 April 2025. https://www.therobotreport.com/figure-ai-ships-figure-02-humanoid-robots-paying-customer/.

Priya Wolf. "Humanoid Robots: Mimicking Human Characteristics and Interactions." *Hakia*. Accessed 7 April 2025. https://hakia.com/humanoid-robots-mimicking-human-characteristics-and-interactions/.

Robert Long et al. "Taking AI Welfare Seriously." *arXiv*. Last modified 4 November 2024. https://arxiv.org/abs/2411.00986.

OpenAI. "GPT-4 System Card." Accessed 7 April 2025. https://cdn.openai.com/papers/gpt-4-system-card.pdf.

OpenAI. "ChatGPT Release Notes." Accessed 7 April 2025. https://help.openai.com/en/articles/6825453-chatgpt-release-notes.

Elizabeth King, Kate Norbury and David Rooney. "Coaching for Leadership Wisdom." *Organizational Dynamics* 51, (2), (2022): 1–10.

Sam Altman. "Reflections." Accessed 7 April 2025. https://blog.samaltman.com/reflections.

Robert J. Sternberg. "A Balance Theory of Wisdom." *Review of General Psychology* 2, (4), (1998): 347–365.

Aristotle. *Nicomachean Ethics*. Translated by H.G. Apostle. Grinnell, IA: The Peripatetic Press, 1984.

Claire Pedrick. *Simplifying Coaching: How to Have More Transformational Conversations by Doing Less*. London: McGraw-Hill Education, 2020.

EMCC Global. "EMCC Global Professional Practice Framework for Mentors, Coaches, and Leaders." 2024.

CHAPTER 4

Stephen M. Walker. "Everything We Know About GPT-4." *Klu.ai Blog*. Last modified 1 September 2024. https://klu.ai/blog/gpt-4-llm.

Britney Muller. "BERT 101: State of the Art NLP Model Explained." Accessed 15 April 2025. https://huggingface.co/blog/bert-101.

Meta. "Introducing Meta Llama 3." Accessed 15 April 2025. https://ai.meta.com/blog/meta-llama-3/.

Jinhyuk Lee et al. "BioBERT: A Pre-trained Biomedical Language Representation Model for Biomedical Text Mining." *Bioinformatics* 36, (4), (2020): 1234–1240. https://doi.org/10.1093/bioinformatics/btz682.

Times of India. "NVIDIA CEO Jensen Huang Challenges AI Assumptions Following DeepSeek Success: 'Almost The Entire World Got It Wrong.'" Accessed 15 April 2025. http://timesofindia.indiatimes.com/articleshow/119181503.cms.

Sharon Goldman. "Nvidia CEO Jensen Huang: AI Will Need More Computing Power." *Fortune.* Last modified 19 March 2025. https://fortune.com/2025/03/19/nvidia-ceo-jensen-huang-ai-will-need-more-computing-power/.

Derek Saul. "Biggest Market Loss in History: NVIDIA Stock Sheds Nearly $600 billion as DeepSeek Shakes AI Darling." *Forbes.* Last modified 27 January 2025. https://www.forbes.com/sites/dereksaul/2025/01/27/biggest-market-loss-in-history-nvidia-stock-sheds-nearly-600-billion-as-deepseek-shakes-ai-darling/.

Pablo Villalobos et al. "Will we Run Out of Data? Limits of LLM Scaling Based on Human-generated Data." *arXiv.* Last modified 4 June 2024. https://arxiv.org/abs/2211.04325.

Maya Williams. "Five Fascinating Facts About The Greek God Apollo." *History Press.* Accessed 15 April 2025. https://thehistorypress.co.uk/article/five-fascinating-facts-about-the-greek-god-apollo/.

Wikipedia. "Apollo." Accessed 15 April 2025. https://en.wikipedia.org/wiki/Apollo.

The Greek gods. "Apollo." Accessed 15 April 2025. https://www.thegreekgods.org/apollo/.

Julian Togelius. *Artificial General Intelligence. MIT Press Essential Knowledge Series.* Cambridge, MA: MIT Press, 2024.

Wikipedia. "Bibliotheca Alexandrina." Accessed 15 April 2025. https://en.wikipedia.org/wiki/Bibliotheca_Alexandrina.

Patrick Haluptzok et al. "Language Models Can Teach Themselves to Program Better." *arXiv.* Last modified 12 April 2023. https://arxiv.org/abs/2207.14502.

Ilia Shumailov et al. "The Curse of Recursion: Training on Generated Data Makes Models Forget." *arXiv.* Last modified 14 April 2023. https://arxiv.org/abs/2305.17493.

CHAPTER 5

University of Hong Kong. "AI in Higher Education." Accessed 21 April 2025. https://web.edu.hku.hk/research_stories/ai-in-higher-education.

Encyclopaedia Britannica. "Industrial Revolution." Accessed 21 April 2025. https://www.britannica.com/event/Industrial-Revolution.

Financial Times. "Liang Wenfeng, the DeepSeek Founder Panicking the Tech World." 31 January 2025. https://www.ft.com/content/b3668e7f-ab8d-473a-9358-12421382cca9.

Xiao Bi et al. "DeepSeek LLM: Scaling Open-Source Language Models with Longtermism." *arXiv.* Last modified 5 January 2024. https://arxiv.org/abs/2401.02954.

Financial Times. "The Global AI Race: Is China Catching Up to the US?" 3 April 2025. https://www.ft.com/content/0e8d6f24-6d45-4de0-b209-8f2130341bae.

Shirin Ghaffary. "OpenAI Finalizes $40 Billion Funding at $300 Billion Value." *Bloomberg.* Last modified 31 March 2025. https://www.bloomberg.com/news/articles/2025-03-31/openai-finalizes-40-billion-funding-at-300-billion-valuation.

Sharon Goldman. "Why OpenAI Caved to Open-source on the Same Day as its $300 Billion Flex." *Fortune.* Last modified 1 April 2025. https://fortune.com/2025/04/01/openai-300m-ghibli-meme-open-source-ai-model-deepseek/.

McKinsey & Company. "The Case for Human-centered AI." Last modified 20 December 2024. https://www.mckinsey.com/capabilities/mckinsey-digital/our-insights/the-case-for-human-centered-ai.

Penelope Campling. "Reforming the Culture of Healthcare: The Case for Intelligent Kindness." BJPsych Bulletin 39 (2015): 1–5. https://doi.org/10.1192/pb.bp.114.047449.

BLURB

Business professionals are facing a tectonic disruption in their industry with the advent of generative artificial intelligence (AI). AI is not only bringing automation to business processes but also has the agency to make critical business decisions. Endowed with a higher level of cognitive ability, AI is able to process more data and make better judgments with the insights from the data.

Much like Pandora's innocent act of opening her box, a gift from Zeus, business leaders are at the precipice of opening the AI box as presented to them. Through the retelling of Zeus, his once trusted ally Prometheus, his trusted son Hephaestus and his enigmatic daughter Athena, business professionals will regain control of the disruption brought upon by AI.

The aim of *Pandora's Pivot* is to help business professionals gain adequate technical depth and understanding of the practical application of AI, to give them an advantage to lead in an AI-driven world.

AUTHOR BIOGRAPHY

Ivan Yong is an author, engineer, organizational psychologist, coach and researcher, who possesses a rare blend of technical expertise and business acumen, uniquely positioning him to demystify AI for business professionals in an AI-driven world.

Currently pursuing a PhD at the University of Nottingham, Malaysia, his research on AI and coaching merges cutting-edge technology with a profound understanding of organizational and human behaviour. His academic foundation includes an MSc in organizational psychology from Birkbeck College, University of London, and an engineering degree from Nanyang Technological University, Singapore, equipping him with the distinctive capability to translate complex scientific concepts into practical solutions.

Ivan is a recognized authority in open innovation, leadership and sales coaching, with a career dedicated to empowering business professionals to achieve transformative business goals. Over the last two decades, he has helped multinationals and startups build multi-million dollar businesses from the ground up, a wealth of experience he translates into actionable insights through his acclaimed books.

His debut book, *Department of Startup: Why Every Fortune 500 Should Have One*, by BEP, New York can be found in 6 of the top 10 global universities (QS World University Rankings, 2026). His latest book, *The Pharaoh's Pitch: Unearthing Ancient Egyptian Wisdom for Sales Success* was longlisted for the UK Business Book Award 2025.

He also regularly publishes books and case studies for Routledge, Taylor & Francis and SAGE Publishing.

A firm believer in unlocking potential in individuals and organizations through coaching and mentoring, Ivan volunteers as the Board Member & Co-President of the European Mentoring & Coaching Council (EMCC), Asia Pacific Region and the Head of Global Social Initiatives with EMCC Global.

Reach out and connect with Ivan Yong on his LinkedIn page (www.linkedin.com/in/ivanyongweikitnaz) or through his Instagram (Instagram.com/ivanyongweikit).